WRITING LYRICS IN A GRID

NOMI YAH

Writing Lyrics In A Grid

Author:	Nomi Yah
Publisher:	Nomi Yah Music PO Box 42, El Verano, CA 95433 NomiYahMusic@gmail.com
Book Design:	Nomi Yah
Cover Art:	Barbara Ann Klatt
Cover Photo:	Mike Lounibos LounibosPhotography.com
Interior Art:	Malaika Wanag
Interior Photos:	Mike Lounibos Ashton Boni Peter Salmon
Title:	Writing Lyrics In A Grid
Distributor:	KDP Publishing
ISBN:	9798518677197

Dedicated to Nicole Milner

Songwriter, composer, musician

My mother and music teacher

My biggest fan and greatest inspiration

CONTENTS

ACKNOWLEDGEMENTS

This book was made possible by my cowriters and music teachers who taught me everything, you know who you are. When reading this book, you may recognize songwriting tips you remember teaching me. If you weren't acknowledged, it isn't because I forgot your contribution, but because I learned from too many of you to name. I appreciate you immensely and I'm deeply grateful for your generosity in sharing your artistry and talent with me.

CHAPTER 1
ORIGIN OF WRITING LYRICS IN A GRID

Writing lyrics in a grid is a method developed over decades of songwriting. It has had a significant impact on my writing ability. I invented the system to solve phrasing problems and make songs more memorable. Writing lyrics in a grid is unlike any other technique of writing lyrics. It has been my tightly guarded secret until now.

My background is a lifetime of songwriting. When I was four-years-old, my mom taught me to read music and the alphabet at the same time. At eight-years-old, I wrote my first song and began performing. At thirteen, I co-wrote King of Kings, leading to my first publishing deal. The song was recorded by Petra on the album Petra Praise: The Rock Cries Out. The album went to the top of the charts for over a year and nearly twenty years later earned a gold record. I got a check large enough to pay for a brand-new Toyota Corolla. The checks still come and the car still runs.

When I was nineteen, I became a professional musician. I performed with dozens of bands and toured internationally. One of my achievements was performing an original song for over one hundred thousand people at a festival in Cabo San Lucas. Another highlight was playing keyboards on a national tour with Eek-A-Mouse and co-writing Prison, released on the Eeksperience album.

I wrote extensively about my adventures in the music business in Notes To Notes: How I Went From Music To Real Estate. It includes stories about attending Jello Biafra's wedding, hosting a Black Flag sleepover, giving a ride to Charles Manson, renting a practice room to Chris Isaac, organizing archives for Daniel Ellsberg, and more. The book is also about real estate and entrepreneurship. If any of it sounds intriguing, the book and audiobook, which I narrated, are available online.

After more than twenty-five years in music, I got off the road to devote myself to being a single mom. Having decided not to perform for a living anymore, I needed to increase my songwriting income. Up until that time, I didn't have formal music education, other than childhood piano lessons and high school band classes. I'd been writing every day since my first song, but never studied the craft or read any books on the subject.

Neglect wasn't the reason I'd avoided studying songwriting for all those years. It was an intentional decision. I actively avoided the influence of teachers because I was determined to develop my own original style and not copy anyone. But when I decided to make a living by songwriting alone, without performing, I had to up my game and write competitively. The songs had to stand on their own, not lean on my ability to entertain.

Being primarily self-taught, I had always studied songs. I had a daily practice of learning new songs, writing out chord charts by ear and playing multiple parts. Woodshedding fortified my ability to have a good career, the equivalent of an athlete working out between games to get an edge on the competition. But all the preparation didn't fully equip me to take on the music publishing industry.

The first time I sat down with a Nashville publisher, I brought him Worth It, a well-received song from my album Get 2 Nomi.

LISTEN
YouTube Channel: Nomi Yah
Playlist: Writing Lyrics In A Grid
Song: Worth It

Link: https://youtu.be/TTkfZFpkuV8
Lyrics: Appendix 3, page 297

The publisher put the CD in his stereo system and the first line of the song sang out, "I don't want to tell you doubts I have in me". The publisher leaned forward and shut the deck off, saying he didn't like the song. I was stunned, asking him how could he dismiss it after only hearing the first 10 seconds. He told me he didn't like the beginning line, "I don't want to tell you". As he explained, if I don't want to tell him, he doesn't want to listen.

He didn't have to be so mean but he was actually very typical in the highly critical arena of industry gatekeepers. It took only a few such stinging critiques to realize I needed to know much more about how publishers judged songs before pitching to them. I'd had a lengthy career, entertaining countless thousands of fans. But the publishers didn't listen to music like fans. These guys, who usually had no musical talent, knew something I didn't know. My competitive spirit slunk off in defeat and vowed to return victorious.

I made a commitment to extensively study the craft of songwriting and master every existing technique. I threw myself into student mode, reading every book I could find and spending hundreds of hours in online research. I attended music conferences and educational events. My first conference was the first year of the ASCAP Expo in Los Angeles. I went to multiple conferences and events hosted by ASCAP, NSAI, Taxi Music and many others. I volunteered with West Coast Songwriters for over a decade, hosting monthly competitions and managing song screenings at the annual convention. Attending so many events with publishers exposed me to their thinking and I began to gain a better understanding of how music was evaluated.

In all that education, what improved my writing the most was working with cowriters, who had standards as high as mine. Their comments, tempered by camaraderie and trust, were relentlessly honest. They tore apart every word I wrote and every new idea I had. I welcomed the challenge and treasured gaining fresh viewpoints. My goal was to learn everything and I was delighted to discover a glorious treasure trove of tips and tricks.

I'd always had raw talent and now the hard work was having the effect of making my writing become well-crafted. Previously, I'd been afraid of teachers somehow stamping themselves on me, dimming my unique artistry. But I got over this fallacy and realized I'm not that delicate. Who I am as an artist is who I am and nobody can infringe on my innate talent. I don't copy teachers just because I learn from them. Knowledge doesn't impose, it only adds polish.

It would be too lengthy to give tribute to all the teachers who contributed to my development. There are hundreds of valuable books and courses. For a taste, I'll give just three bits of wisdom distilled from a deluge of information.

I met Eric Bazilian (One Of Us) at a conference in Los Angeles. In his workshop he said every good song has a "nugget of genius". It can be anything, a melody, a phrase or an instrumental hook. His tip was to identify the nugget and repeat it, to make a song catchier.

I took a course from Steve Seskin (Grown Men Don't Cry) held in his living room. His advice was to save one note in the melody for the hook, a note that isn't being used in the rest of the song. He also said to be aware of where a phrase starts, whether the first syllable is before, on or after the downbeat. His techniques can be used to create a sharper contrast between song sections.

I read Writing Better Lyrics by Pat Pattison (Berklee School Of Music) and met the author. In one of the chapters, he describes a method of generating lyrics to support the core message of a song and eliminate writer's block. First identify the main theme in a single word and look it up in a thesaurus. Next find other words resonating with the message and look those words up. Follow each interesting thread, creating a list of words, then look up each word in a rhyming dictionary. In a short time, this will generate a ton of fresh ideas relevant to the main theme.

These tips are only three examples of the many lessons I learned. Whenever I picked up a new tip, I tried it out on a song. If it worked well, I put it in my tool belt and integrated it into my writing style. No doubt about it, my songwriting improved tremendously. Storylines became stronger and word choices got more interesting. I was in love with rewriting. I wrote and rewrote and relentlessly rewrote again. Amateur cowriters had tortured looks on their faces and ghosted me. Professional cowriters were magnetized by the results.

But even with all that education, I kept finding phrasing issues. Something would feel off, a line didn't precisely fit into a melody, some lyrics seemed cluttered and weren't in the groove. I couldn't find a system to organize the muddled words, even with all the tools of the trade. When it came to phrasing, I had to rely entirely on instinct and chance.

The idea for writing lyrics in a grid had its origin in my childhood, when counting beats fascinated me. Every time I heard a song, I counted in time to the rhythm. My parents had hundreds of records and I counted along to Beethoven, Beatles and Bulgarian throat singers alike. The genre didn't matter, counting revealed a common element: one-two-three-four. We lived way out in the country, without a television or nearby friends, and I filled my days playing music. I spent so many hours playing in time to a metronome, I earned the nickname Metronomi.

The childhood game of counting beats led directly to the development, decades later, of writing lyrics in a grid. I was in the midst of writing a song, which had one really good sentence followed by an awkward sentence. I liked the second line, but it wasn't in the pocket. The lyrics weren't locked into the rhythm and I couldn't figure out why. I rewrote the troublesome line over and over, each time like a shot in the dark. I came up with plenty of alternative lyrics, using intuition and chance, not skill and craft. No matter what I did, I couldn't match the first sentence with an equally good second sentence. I didn't know what to do except keep tossing out ideas, hoping one would fit better.

As I focused my attention on the issue, I couldn't pinpoint what was off in a precise way. I needed to see it more clearly to solve the problem. If only I had a map to look at it visually. A map? What was I thinking? I cut small squares of paper and wrote one syllable on each piece. I lined up the pieces of paper on the table to form the two sentences. When I saw the syllables lined up, I instantly had a feeling I was on to something. The number of syllables in each sentence was the same, but one fit the melody and one didn't. I couldn't identify what was wrong accurately until I knew precisely where each syllable belonged.

I always have stenographer notebooks; I buy them by the dozen. A pen hooks into the spiral binding and the width of paper is exactly right for a line of lyrics. I took out a steno pad and opened it to a blank page. There was a line going down the center, dividing the page into two columns. I drew another line down the center of each column and created four columns. I drew lines down the center of each of those columns and made eight columns. I had made a grid with eight boxes in a row, corresponding to the eight beats in a bar.

I took the pieces of paper with individual syllables and put each into the box on the beat where it belonged. When both sentences were laid out in the grid, I compared the good sentence to the troublesome one. There it was in front of me. I could clearly see the problem visually in the patterns. A few syllables weren't matching neatly, the phrasing was haphazard. Up until this point, I could hear the problem. Suddenly, I could see it.

I moved a couple of syllables and, bingo, the song clicked into alignment. Just like that! I didn't rewrite the awkward sentence. All I did was move a few syllables a little and the result was undeniable. The subtle adjustment in phrasing resulted in an astonishing improvement. I tried the method with another song and another, honing the technique.

Accurate phrasing had been an ongoing problem. With the invention of writing lyrics in a grid, I finally had a solution. Once I figured it out, the method had a powerful impact on my songwriting. I tested songs out on industry professionals and the new material received consistently high praise and publishing deals. I especially valued the feedback from professional songwriters:

- "Cool rhymes, very strong, courageous and creative." Pat and Pete Luboff (Patti LaBelle, Snoop Dogg)
- "Great writing, solid chorus, verses very, very strong." Rich E. Blaze (Diane Warren, Rod Stewart, Timbaland)
- "Lyrics made me say Wow! Knocked me out!" Pamela Phillips-Oland (Whitney Houston, Frank Sinatra, Reba McIntyre)
- "This song is a masterpiece." Larry Batiste (Michael Bolton, Whitney Houston)
- "Absolutely gorgeous melody!" Jai Josefs (Jose Feliciano, Little Richard)
- "Really cool idea, lyrics are whoa!" Steve Seskin (Tim McGraw, Kenny Chesney)

After a few years of using my new technique, I came to notice I was the only songwriter writing lyrics in a grid. In all the education I went through, there wasn't anything about using visual patterns to analyze songs, nothing even close. It dawned on me that I'd developed a truly unique method of lyric writing and I coined the term "syllabalizing".

I considered syllabalizing to be a trade secret and didn't tell anyone about it for a long time. I only showed it to one or two people ever. After years of carefully keeping it covert, it began to feel like too good of a technique to keep to myself. I was in the process of publishing a songbook and decided to include actual grids from writing sessions. I snuck the grids into the graphics (Appendix 5, page 313) and in this quiet way revealed my secret. I waited for its anticipated impact on the songwriting community, but my subtle revelation went unnoticed. Not even one person commented on the grids, everyone assumed they were only graphics.

Writing lyrics in a grid has been my secret weapon, developed and kept under wraps for many years. It has given me an edge in the tough music business. Being competitive is all well and good, but I can no longer see the point of secrecy. We don't take anything with us, the best we can do is leave something behind. So here it is, a book about writing lyrics in a grid.

I don't blame you if you're skeptical about the idea of writing lyrics in a grid. Maybe you believe songs turn out better when they're spontaneous, not studiously crafted. Your position would have validity, it's certainly true that craft without inspiration rings hollow. But the most effective combination is inspiration polished by craft.

Do you think being over-analytical will crush your artistry? Maybe your concern, as a songwriter, is to protect your individuality and nurture your own raw creativity. I assure you, using a grid won't diminish your brilliance, it's just a tool to fine-tune ideas. Looking at lyric patterns gives you the ability to see misaligned syllables, but it's your choice to edit or keep the variations.

I've used the technique of writing lyrics in a grid to polish rough drafts for many an artist. Great performers often lack extensive writing skills, even when they are talented and inspired, and most major artists have a songwriting team. If your goal is to be on the same level as a professional songwriting team, Writing Lyrics In A Grid will teach you a valuable tool you won't learn anywhere else.

This book isn't for beginners, the material is for advanced songwriters in pursuit of honing their craft. For those of you starting out, I recommend reading Writing Better Lyrics by Pat Pattison and Tunesmith by Jimmy Webb. These two books will give you a great launch into songwriting.

For those who are already dedicated songwriters, I hope you find this method adds value. For anyone interested in music appreciation, Writing Lyrics In A Grid offers a fascinating viewpoint, a plunge into the deep end of lyric craft.

It feels counter-intuitive to write this book knowing it won't be particularly entertaining, or even slightly interesting, to the vast majority of readers. But I can't figure out how to share the information without going into methodical detail. I have to write a technical manual. If mass appeal isn't motivating me to write, what is? Writing Lyrics In A Grid is written for committed songwriters and obsessed music scholars, who may enjoy learning an innovative way to understand lyrics.

As you progress methodically, fully understanding each step before going on to the next, you'll quickly realize that syllabalizing is a very simple technique. There are only a few things to master and you'll have it down. Stick with me, repeating the steps as needed, and you'll conquer the small learning curve and gain an indispensable tool.

CHAPTER 2
EXPLANATION OF WRITING LYRICS IN A GRID

The basic method of writing lyrics in a grid is simple, with only two steps. The grid has eight boxes in each row. The eight boxes correspond to eight beats of music.

1	2	3	4	5	6	7	8

First step, tap your finger on each box from left to right, and sing in time. For each syllable you sing, your finger is touching a box. Write the syllable you are singing into the box you are touching.

Second step, when all the syllables are laid out in the grid, look at the patterns. You can see exactly where there is too much variation or not enough. Writing lyrics in a grid is like having a microscope that enables you to rewrite with precision.

If you're like most songwriters, you've had the experience of writing a lyric that's almost working, but not quite. If it ends up in the final version, every time the line plays, it'll bother you, even when nobody else notices. There can be many reasons a lyric doesn't feel right, it might be story content, word choice, or melody. There are ample techniques to address these issues. But sometimes there are lyrics that, even after diligent rewriting, still don't feel quite right. You can hear there's a problem, but you can't put your finger on it. When you're writing in a grid, you're tapping the boxes and literally putting your finger on it!

Writing lyrics in a grid is a technique to solve the problem of awkward phrasing. It allows you to see a visual aspect of lyrics, using your eyes to analyze audio patterns. It gives you conscious control over the exact rhythmic placement of each syllable. Songwriters often aren't aware of the rhythmic placement of syllables, relying on instinct alone. Even professionals can get stuck with a slightly-off sentence. If you can't see exactly what's wrong, you can't figure out how to fix it. That's where syllabalizing comes in and it's a powerful tool.

Songwriting is an artistic balance between repetition and variation. There are places in a song where you choose repetition and other places where you choose variation. Skilled use of repetition and variation in melody and phrasing is a hallmark of memorable songwriting. It isn't surprising repetition improves memorability, it's how all skills are learned. Repetition is used in marketing to create name recognition. Repetition builds the muscles of athletes, ensures the reliability of science, and deepens the practice of religion.

Writing lyrics in a grid is a method allowing you to visually see patterns and gain accurate control over the critical elements of repetition and variation. By writing lyrics in a grid, you can literally see a problem. You can analyze patterns clearly and choose repetition and variation intentionally. You can pinpoint where a variation is subtly jarring or a line is dully repetitive.

In addition to being a songwriting technique, syllabalizing is an excellent way to analyze existing songs. I've deconstructed countless songs in grids. It helps me understand the elements that make me sing along or provoke an emotional response. It shows me exactly what is happening when part of a song gets stuck in my head. Syllabalizing quantifies a sphere of phrasing and melody, exposing precisely what is great about a great song.

Using well-known songs is the simplest way to explain how syllabalizing works. But the legal restrictions and permissions are daunting. So, I'm using my original songs instead, and some in the public domain, to demonstrate the method. The familiarity of the public domain songs makes it easier to grasp the concepts of writing lyrics in a grid. The original songs offer an in-depth view of how writing in a grid enhances creativity.

There are eight boxes for eight beats, write each syllable in its corresponding box and analyze patterns. In one sentence, that's how you write lyrics in a grid. But the technique is deceptively simple, there's a learning curve to grasping this unfamiliar method of songwriting. You're used to hearing musical patterns, not seeing them. We'll proceed methodically, with granular slowness at the beginning. As you get used to applying the method, we'll gradually speed up and abbreviate the process.

If you are a music producer, you're already used to visual patterns of audio in a grid. In music production software, each horizontal row is an individual track and each vertical line marks a beat. When a note is in the wrong location, you can simultaneously hear and see it. You can physically move notes into alignment. Writing lyrics in a grid is the same concept applied to lyrics.

If you can read music, you're already used to visual patterns of audio in a grid. Each horizontal line, and the space between lines, corresponds to a note in a scale and each vertical line marks a beat. Written notes reveal audio patterns visually in a grid. If you apply the concept to lyrics, you'll have no difficulty learning how to write lyrics in a grid.

Historically, the first known grid was a seven-thousand-year-old ledger found in Mesopotamia. In 1794, Dr. Buxton of England got the patent for paper printed with a rectangular coordinate grid. Music makes use of grids for music production and manuscripts. But writing lyrics in a grid is the first technique to use grids for lyric writing.

CHAPTER 3
TOOLS FOR WRITING LYRICS IN A GRID

Writing lyrics in a grid is a highly streamlined method. You'll learn all the details and it isn't complicated. The technique in a nutshell is simple:
- Write syllables in a grid
- Look at patterns

That's it, that's all there is to writing lyrics in a grid.

The only tools you need to get started are a grid and three symbols.

THE GRID

The grid has eight boxes in each row. The eight boxes correspond to eight beats of music.

1	2	3	4	5	6	7	8

Syllabalizing works in alternate time as well. For example, in 3/4 time, the grid has six boxes in each row, corresponding to six beats of music.

1	2	3	4	5	6

There are several easy ways to make the grids themselves. Find the way that works best for you.

STENOGRAPHER NOTEBOOK

Steno pads are spiral-bound on top and the paper is ruled. There's a vertical line down the middle, forming two columns.

Draw two additional lines, splitting each of the two columns in half, creating four columns.

Draw four additional lines, splitting each of the four columns in half, creating eight columns.

For a song in 3/4 time, draw four lines, splitting each of the two columns in thirds, creating six columns.

RULED PAPER

Using ruled paper, draw a line down the center and create two columns.

Draw two lines, splitting each of the two columns in half, creating four columns.

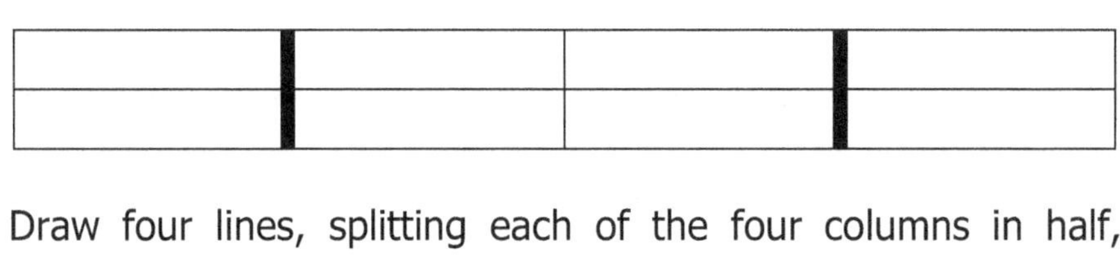

Draw four lines, splitting each of the four columns in half, creating eight columns.

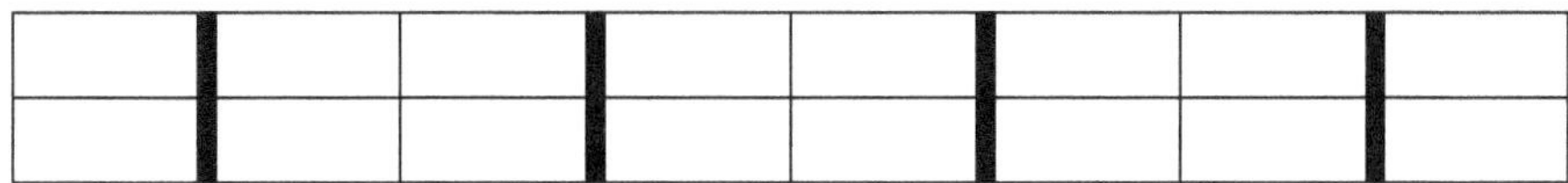

For a song in 3/4 time, draw a line down the center, creating two columns.

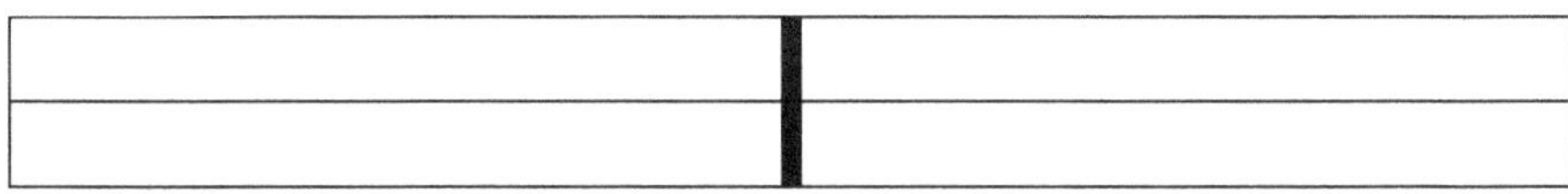

Draw four lines, split each of the two columns in thirds, creating six columns.

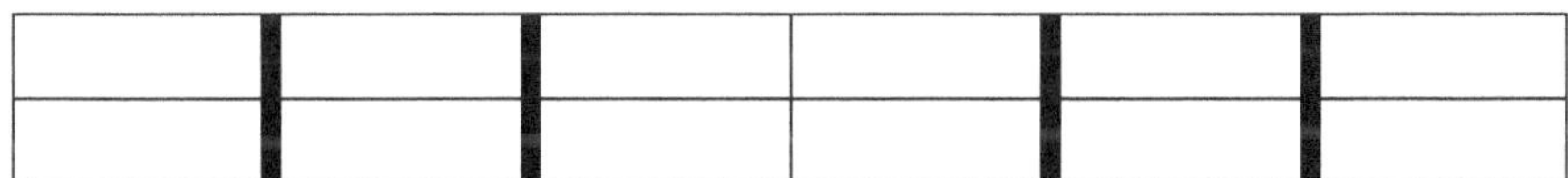

DOCUMENT

These are the directions in my version of Word. Your computer software may be different, with other steps to insert a table.

Insert > Table > New Insert Table > Columns 8 > Rows 3 (or more) > Autofit To Window > OK

GRAPH PAPER

It couldn't be much easier to create a grid than to use a preprinted grid on graph paper. The columns and rows are already there. Use eight of the columns for eight beats.

SPREADSHEET

It's simple to create a grid using a spreadsheet on a computer. The columns and rows are already there. Use columns A through H for the eight columns.

TWO HANDS

It's possible to syllabalize without paper and pen or computer, using just your fingers. This is an advanced technique because you aren't able to use your eyes to look at patterns. But after enough practice it isn't difficult to do in your head. You'll be able to solve songwriting problems on the fly with no supplies, other than your hands.

Your eight fingers correspond to the eight boxes in a row and your thumbs are for tapping. Put your hands in front of you, palms facing down and fingers spread. Imagine your fingers are the grid, with four boxes on the right hand and four boxes on the left hand. Use your thumbs to touch your fingers from left to right, as though tapping the eight boxes of the grid.
   1. Left thumb touch left pinky
   2. Left thumb touch left ring finger
   3. Left thumb touch left middle finger
   4. Left thumb touch left index finger
   5. Right thumb touch right index finger
   6. Right thumb touch right middle finger
   7. Right thumb touch right ring finger
   8. Right thumb touch right pinky

ONE HAND

This is the most advanced way to syllabalize. When I was a child entertaining myself by counting beats, I came up with this way of counting to eight on one hand. It's a trick I've always used, but never told anyone about until now. With one hand, tap on any surface. Tapping can be a subtle movement, done silently without anyone noticing. It makes you look like a genius in a cowriting session!

Tap all the fingers on one hand, including the thumb.
1. Tap thumb
2. Tap index finger
3. Tap middle finger
4. Tap ring finger
5. Tap pinky
6. Tap ring finger
7. Tap middle finger
8. Tap index finger

MIND

You can't get a much sparser technique than tapping fingers of one hand. But actually, there is an even less active way to make a grid. Visualize a grid, seeing and hearing lyrics in the squares of your mind. If you see me staring off into space, and wonder what I'm thinking, this may be a clue.

The fact is, it's normal for skilled songwriters to work out phrasing in their mind. But this book explains how to do it consciously, instead of just instinctively.

PRINTER

Put the following page on your printer and make copies of the blank grid.

THE SYMBOLS

Writing lyrics in a grid involves placing individual syllables in the boxes of a grid. We want every syllable to be on a corresponding beat of music. But some boxes don't have a syllable in them, otherwise there would be non-stop rapid-fire syllables, one on each beat.

For a beat without a syllable, the corresponding box isn't empty. The music doesn't stop between syllables and we're charting all of it. There are three symbols used to fill in a box with no syllable.

SYMBOL "x"

"x" (ex) is used when there's an empty space in the words. When a singer takes one or more beats without singing a syllable, the corresponding boxes are filled with an "x".

SYMBOL "-"

"-" (dash) is a held over note. During a performance, sung notes are held over all the time. But for the sake of understanding patterns, we only use this symbol when a syllable changes to another note. When a syllable is held over for two or more notes, the boxes with the held over notes are filled with a "-".

SYMBOL "___"

"___" (underline) is used when there's a double syllable in a box. In syncopated phrasing, when there are two syllables in one box, the syllables are underlined with a "___".

CHAPTER 4
WRITE A LULLABY
IN A GRID

The best way to explain how to write lyrics in a grid is to demonstrate the process, step by step. We'll start with a song from the public domain, one of the simplest lullabies ever written, Mary Had A Little Lamb.

The basic technique is to tap your finger inside the boxes and sing with the rhythm, the same way you'd tap your foot in time to a song.

First, put your finger on the top left box of the grid. Tap your finger inside each of the grid boxes, from left to right. In time with the tapping, count from one to eight.

Tap from left to right and count from one to eight. Touch the number at the same time you say the number.

1	2	3	4	5	6	7	8

Tapping and counting out loud from one to eight seems too simplistic. But I urge you to try it anyway because it is the basis of writing lyrics in a grid. We'll build on this humble beginning and gradually grow in complexity.

LEARN THE SONG

Most people remember Mary Had A Little Lamb from early childhood. For a quick reminder, take a moment to learn the song. We'll only work on the first verse since all the verses are similar.

We'll be referring to specific lines in the lyrics. Here is a reference guide to the line numbers.

SONG
Mary Had A Little Lamb (Lowell Mason)

LINE NUMBERS
VERSE 1, LINE 1: Mary had a little lamb
VERSE 1, LINE 2: Little lamb, little lamb
VERSE 1, LINE 3: Mary had a little lamb
VERSE 1, LINE 4: Its fleece was white as snow
VERSE 1, LINE 5: And everywhere that Mary went
VERSE 1, LINE 6: Mary went, Mary went
VERSE 1, LINE 7: Everywhere that Mary went
VERSE 1, LINE 8: The lamb was sure to go

LISTEN
YouTube Channel: Nomi Yah
Playlist: Writing Lyrics In A Grid
Song: Mary Had A Little Lamb
Link: https://youtu.be/2Vg_yfcAsfY
Lyrics: Appendix 3, page 288

STEP 1

Begin with the first line, Verse 1, Line 1. Write the lyrics in the grid slowly, one box at a time, until you get the hang of it. After the first line is in the grid, look at it closely and identify patterns.

Tap from left to right on the top row. At the same time, count from one to eight. Your finger is touching the number at the same time you speak it.

1	2	3	4	5	6	7	8

Continue to tap evenly and replace the numbers with lyrics. In time with the tapping, sing Verse 1, Line 1. Your finger is tapping left to right, touching each of the eight boxes in Row 1, while you sing.

VERSE 1, LINE 1: Mary had a little lamb

What box is your finger touching on the first syllable "Mar"? The first syllable "Mar" is on the downbeat.

Row 1, Box 1 = "Mar"

Mar							

Start over. Tap your finger from the top, from left to right, eight taps each row, singing Verse 1, Line 1 again. Double-check your finger is touching Row 1, Box 1 "Mar" at the same moment you are singing it. If not, go back to the beginning of this step and review the instructions before continuing on.

What box is your finger touching on the second syllable "y"? The second syllable "y" is on the second beat.

Row 1, Box 2 = "y"

Mar	y						

Start over from the top. What box is your finger touching on the next syllable "had"? "Had" is on the third beat.

Row 1, Box 3 = "had"

Mar	y	had					

What box is your finger touching on the next word "a"?

Row 1, Box 4 = "a"

Mar	y	had	a				

The next word has two syllables "little".

Row 1, Box 5 = "lit"
Row 1, Box 6 = "tle"

Mar	y	had	a	lit	tle		

Keep going, repeating the process and filling in the grid.

Row 1, Box 7 = "lamb"

Mar	y	had	a	lit	tle	lamb	

Writing lyrics in a grid only requires repeating two actions:
1. Write syllables in a grid
2. Look at patterns

You've completed the first action, writing Verse 1, Line 1 in a grid. Next complete the second action and look at the patterns.

IDENTIFY PATTERNS

Look at the pattern of the first line. Write down what you notice about the pattern. Note anything of creative interest, like rhymes or alliteration.

Mar	y	had	a	lit	tle	lamb	

Row 1, Boxes 5 and 7 have alliteration "little" and "lamb".

Notice the pattern of syllables in consecutive boxes. Row 1, Boxes 1, 2, 3, 4, 5, 6 and 7 each have one syllable.
This is what a lullaby looks like. It has a straightforward pattern even a small child can learn.

STEP 2

Writing lyrics in a grid can be confusing at first. If you're at all lost so far, go back and repeat the previous step. Understanding Step 1 will make Step 2 much easier.

Ready? Move on to the next line, Verse 1, Line 2. Syllabalize slowly, box by box, then identify patterns. Start over from the top left corner. Tap your finger in each box, from left to right, and sing in time.

VERSE 1, LINE 2: Little lamb, little lamb

What box is your finger touching when you sing the first word "little"? The first syllable "lit" is on the downbeat, in Row 2, Box 1. That means Row 1, Box 8 doesn't have a syllable in it. Write the symbol "x" to signify the box is empty.

Row 1, Box 8 = "x"

Mar	y	had	a	lit	tle	lamb	x

Row 2, Box 1 = "lit"
Row 2, Box 2 = "tle"

Mar	y	had	a	lit	tle	lamb	x
lit	tle						

What box is your finger touching on the next word "lamb"?

Row 2, Box 3 = "lamb"

Mar	y	had	a	lit	tle	lamb	x
lit	tle	lamb					

Row 2, Box 4 is empty, marked with the symbol "x".

Row 2, Box 4 = "x"

Mar	y	had	a	lit	tle	lamb	x
lit	tle	lamb	x				

What box is your finger touching on the next word "little"?
Row 2, Box 5 = "lit"
Row 2, Box 6 = "tle"

Mar	y	had	a	lit	tle	lamb	x
lit	tle	lamb	x	lit	tle		

What box is your finger touching on "lamb"?

Row 2, Box 7 = "lamb"

Mar	y	had	a	lit	tle	lamb	x
lit	tle	lamb	x	lit	tle	lamb	

IDENTIFY PATTERNS

Put the first two lines in separate grids to make it easier to compare. Look for differences and similarities. Notice rhymes or anything interesting.

Verse 1, Line 1:

Mar	y	had	a	lit	tle	lamb	x

Verse 1, Line 2:

lit	tle	lamb	x	lit	tle	lamb	

Boxes 1, 2 and 3 have the same phrasing, with a syllable in each box.

Boxes 4 have a variation, with Line 1 having a syllable and Line 2 being empty.

The alliteration "little" and "lamb" is repeated three times in the exact same way. Although the melody shifts, the rhythmic pattern and lyrics are identical.

Repetition of phrase and phrasing is one of the reasons even a baby can learn this song.

STEP 3

In this step, continue on to Verse 1, Line 3. Write the lyrics in the correct boxes, then identify patterns.

Tap your finger in each box, from left to right, and sing in time.

VERSE 1, LINE 3: Mary had a little lamb

What box is your finger touching on "Mar"? The first syllable is on the downbeat. This means there's an empty box at the end of the previous line. Write the symbol "x" to signify the box is empty.

Row 2, Box 8 = "x"

Mar	y	had	a	lit	tle	lamb	x
lit	tle	lamb	x	lit	tle	lamb	x

Verse 1, Line 3 is the same as Verse 1, Line 1.

Row 3, Box 1 = "Mar"
Row 3, Box 2 = "y"
Row 3, Box 3 = "had"
Row 3, Box 4 = "a"
Row 3, Box 5 = "lit"
Row 3, Box 6 = "tle"
Row 3, Box 7 = "lamb"

Mar	y	had	a	lit	tle	lamb	x
lit	tle	lamb	x	lit	tle	lamb	x
Mar	y	had	a	lit	tle	lamb	

IDENTIFY PATTERNS

Compare the three lines to each other. Put each line on a separate grid to make the patterns easier to see.

How are the three lines different? How are they similar?

Verse 1: Line 1:

Mar	y	had	a	lit	tle	lamb	x

Verse 1: Line 2:

lit	tle	lamb	x	lit	tle	lamb	x

Verse 1: Line 3:

Mar	y	had	a	lit	tle	lamb	

The phrase "little lamb" is repeated four times in the exact same pattern.

Lines 1 and 3 are identical.

There is only one phrasing variation in the three lines, in Box 4 of Verse 1, Line 2 with an "x" instead of a syllable.

This is classic nursery rhyme fare, repetitive and predictable.

STEP 4

We don't always syllabalize chronologically, as you will see. But for this first example, we'll proceed methodically and work on the following line, Verse 1, Line 4. Write the syllables in the grid and identify patterns.

VERSE 1, LINE 4: Its fleece was white as snow

Begin again from the top, tapping left to right. What box is your finger touching on "its"?

This line is different than the three previous lines because the first syllable isn't on the downbeat. The first word comes in as a pick-up note before the downbeat.

Row 3, Box 8 = "its"

Mar	y	had	a	lit	tle	lamb	x
lit	tle	lamb	x	lit	tle	lamb	x
Mar	y	had	a	lit	tle	lamb	its

Start over. What box is your finger touching on "fleece"? The word is on the downbeat, so your finger is touching Box 1.

Row 4, Box 1 = "fleece"

Mar	y	had	a	lit	tle	lamb	x
lit	tle	lamb	x	lit	tle	lamb	x
Mar	y	had	a	lit	tle	lamb	its
fleece							

Row 4, Box 2 = "was"

Mar	y	had	a	lit	tle	lamb	x
lit	tle	lamb	x	lit	tle	lamb	x
Mar	y	had	a	lit	tle	lamb	its
fleece	was						

Row 4, Box 3 = "white"

Mar	y	had	a	lit	tle	lamb	x
lit	tle	lamb	x	lit	tle	lamb	x

Mar	y	had	a	lit	tle	lamb	its
fleece	was	white					

Row 4, Box 4 = "as"

Mar	y	had	a	lit	tle	lamb	x
lit	tle	lamb	x	lit	tle	lamb	x
Mar	y	had	a	lit	tle	lamb	its
fleece	was	white	as				

Row 4, Box 5 = "snow"

Mar	y	had	a	lit	tle	lamb	x
lit	tle	lamb	x	lit	tle	lamb	x
Mar	y	had	a	lit	tle	lamb	its
fleece	was	white	as	snow			

IDENTIFY PATTERNS

Mar	y	had	a	lit	tle	lamb	x
lit	tle	lamb	x	lit	tle	lamb	x
Mar	y	had	a	lit	tle	lamb	its
fleece	was	white	as	snow			

Rows 1 and 3 are the same, except Row 3, Box 8 has an extra syllable "its".

Row 1, Boxes 5, 6 and 7 "little lamb" is repeated in Row 2, Boxes 1, 2 and 3, also in Row 2, Boxes 5, 6 and 7, and in Row 3, Boxes 5, 6 and 7.

Row 4, Boxes 1, 2, 3, 4 and 5 fill consecutive boxes, matching Rows 1 and 3, Boxes 1, 2, 3, 4 and 5.

Do you think the second four lines of Verse 1 have the same pattern of repetition and variation as the first four lines?

STEP 5

In the previous steps, you worked on the first half of the verse, Lines 1 to 4. In this step, syllabalize the second half of the verse, Lines 5 to 8.

When the second half of the verse is in the grid, compare it to the patterns in the first half. Notice if the patterns are identical or different.

VERSE 1, LINE 5: And everywhere that Mary went

Begin from the top, tapping left to right. What box is your finger touching on the word "and"?

"And" is not on the downbeat. It's a pick-up syllable before the downbeat.

Row 1, Box 8 = "and"

							and

What box is your finger touching on "everywhere"?

Row 2, Box 1 = "eve"
Row 2, Box 2 = "ry"
Row 2, Box 3 = "where"

							and
eve	ry	where					

Row 2, Box 4 = "that"

							and
eve	ry	where	that				

Row 2, Box 5 = "Mar"
Row 2, Box 6 = "y"

							and
eve	ry	where	that	Mar	y		

Row 2, Box 7 = "went"

							and
eve	ry	where	that	Mar	y	went	

IDENTIFY PATTERNS

The first half of the verse begins with Line 1. The second half begins with Line 5. Compare Lines 1 and 5.

Verse 1, Line 1:

Mar	y	had	a	lit	tle	lamb	

Verse 1, Line 5:

							and
eve	ry	where	that	Mar	y	went	

These two lines have all the syllables in the same boxes, except for the pick-up syllable in Verse 1, Line 5 "and".

This shows one variation between the two halves. Continue syllabalizing to find out if there are other variations.

STEP 6

Syllabalize the following line, Verse 1, Line 6. Compare Verse 1, Line 6 with the corresponding Verse 1, Line 2.

VERSE 1, LINE 6: Mary went, Mary went

Begin again from the top, tapping left to right. What box is your finger touching on "Mary"?

The first syllable "Mar" is on the downbeat, in Row 3, Box 1. That means there's an empty beat at the end of the previous line. Write the "x" symbol in Row 2, Box 8.

Row 2, Box 8 = "x"
Row 3, Box 1 = "Mar"
Row 3, Box 2 = "y"

							and
eve	ry	where	that	Mar	y	went	x
Mar	y						

What box is your finger touching when you sing "went"?

Row 3, Box 3 = "went"

							and
eve	ry	where	that	Mar	y	went	x
Mar	y	went					

The next syllable "Mar" is in Box 5, which means Box 4 is empty.

Row 3, Box 4 = "x"
Row 3, Box 5 = "Mar"
Row 3, Box 6 = "y"

							and
eve	ry	where	that	Mar	y	went	x
Mar	y	went	x	Mar	y		

Row 3, Box 7 = "went"

							and
eve	ry	where	that	Mar	y	went	x
Mar	y	went	x	Mar	y	went	

IDENTIFY PATTERNS

Verse 1, Lines 1 & 2:

Mar	y	had	a	lit	tle	lamb	x
lit	tle	lamb	x	lit	tle	lamb	x

Verse 1, Lines 5 & 6:

							and
eve	ry	where	that	Mar	y	went	x
Mar	y	went	x	Mar	y	went	

Other than the pick-up syllable "and", both halves have identical phrasing.

In the second half "Mary went" repeats with the same pattern as in the first half "little lamb".

The only variation is the pick-up "and" in Verse 1, Line 5.

STEP 7

Go on to the next line, Verse 1, Line 7. Identify patterns after you write the syllables in the grid.

VERSE 2, LINE 7: Everywhere that Mary went

What box is your finger touching on "everywhere"? The first syllable "eve" is on the downbeat in Row 4, Box 1. This means the end of the previous line has an empty beat, signified by the symbol "x".

Row 3, Box 8 = "x"
Row 4, Box 1 = "eve"
Row 4, Box 2 = "ry"
Row 4, Box 3 = "where"

							and
eve	ry	where	that	Mar	y	went	x
Mar	y	went	x	Mar	y	went	x
eve	ry	where					

Row 4, Box 4 = "that"

							and
eve	ry	where	that	Mar	y	went	x
Mar	y	went	x	Mar	y	went	x
eve	ry	where	that				

Row 4, Box 5 = "Mar"
Row 4, Box 6 = "y"

							and
eve	ry	where	that	Mar	y	went	x
Mar	y	went	x	Mar	y	went	x
eve	ry	where	that	Mar	y		

Row 4, Box 7 = "went"

							and
eve	ry	where	that	Mar	y	went	x
Mar	y	went	x	Mar	y	went	x
eve	ry	where	that	Mar	y	went	

							and
eve	ry	where	that	Mar	y	went	x
Mar	y	went	x	Mar	y	went	x
eve	ry	where	that	Mar	y	went	

The phrase "Mary went" lines up neatly, just as we saw with "little lamb".

In the first half of the verse, we saw in Line 4 "its fleece was white as snow" how the first syllable is a pick-up before the downbeat. In the second half of the verse, does the corresponding Verse 1, Line 8 "the lamb was sure to go" have the same pick-up?

STEP 8

Does Verse 1, Line 4 "its fleece was white as snow" match Verse 1, Line 8 "the lamb was sure to go"?

Syllabalize Verse 1, Line 8 and compare patterns with Verse 1, Line 4.

VERSE 1, LINE 8: The lamb was sure to go

What box is your finger touching on "the"? It's a pick-up before the downbeat.

Row 4, Box 8 = "the"

							and
eve	ry	where	that	Mar	y	went	x
Mar	y	went	x	Mar	y	went	x
eve	ry	where	that	Mar	y	went	the

What box is your finger touching on "lamb"?

Row 5, Box 1 = "lamb"

							and
eve	ry	where	that	Mar	y	went	x
Mar	y	went	x	Mar	y	went	x
eve	ry	where	that	Mar	y	went	the
lamb							

Row 5, Box 2 = "was"

							and
eve	ry	where	that	Mar	y	went	x
Mar	y	went	x	Mar	y	went	x
eve	ry	where	that	Mar	y	went	the
lamb	was						

Row 5, Box 3 = "sure"

							and
eve	ry	where	that	Mar	y	went	x
Mar	y	went	x	Mar	y	went	x
eve	ry	where	that	Mar	y	went	the
lamb	was	sure					

Row 5, Box 4 = "to"

							and
eve	ry	where	that	Mar	y	went	x
Mar	y	went	x	Mar	y	went	x
eve	ry	where	that	Mar	y	went	the
lamb	was	sure	to				

Row 5, Box 5 = "go"

							and
eve	ry	where	that	Mar	y	went	x
Mar	y	went	x	Mar	y	went	x
eve	ry	where	that	Mar	y	went	the
lamb	was	sure	to	go			

IDENTIFY PATTERNS

Compare the patterns of the first and second halves of Verse 1. What is the same and what is different?

Verse 1, Lines 1 - 4:

Mar	y	had	a	lit	tle	lamb	x
lit	tle	lamb	x	lit	tle	lamb	x
Mar	y	had	a	lit	tle	lamb	its
fleece	was	white	as	snow			

Verse 1, Lines 5 - 8:

							and
eve	ry	where	that	Mar	y	went	x
Mar	y	went	x	Mar	y	went	x
eve	ry	where	that	Mar	y	went	the
lamb	was	sure	to	go			

Rows 1 are different because Line 1 starts on the downbeat of Row 2, whereas Line 5 has a pick-up syllable "and" in Row 1.

Other than the variation of the pick-up note, the two halves of the verse have identical phrasing in every box.

The last syllables of the two halves rhyme "snow' and "go".

Rows 2 and 4 repeat in an identical way.

SUMMARY

In Chapter 4, you learned how to:
- Write syllables in a grid
- Identify patterns
- Compare patterns
- Recognize the pattern of a lullaby

The other verses of Mary Had A Little Lamb follow an almost identical pattern to the first. I chose one of the easiest songs ever written to introduce you to the method of writing lyrics in a grid.

Take a look at the verse as a whole.

Verse 1:

Mar	y	had	a	lit	tle	lamb	x
lit	tle	lamb	x	lit	tle	lamb	x
Mar	y	had	a	lit	tle	lamb	its
fleece	was	white	as	snow	x	x	and
eve	ry	where	that	Mar	y	went	x
Mar	y	went	x	Mar	y	went	x
eve	ry	where	that	Mar	y	went	the
lamb	was	sure	to	go			

The simplicity in the patterns is apparent. The syllables line up in consecutive boxes. Repetition is consistent and rhymes are predictable. The phrasing isn't syncopated, there are no complex rhythms.

This is what a lullaby looks like. A lined-up pattern is a signature feature of most lullabies. The same pattern is common in patriotic, religious and folk songs. Have a look at a few examples.

YouTube Channel:	Nomi Yah
Playlist:	Writing Lyrics In A Grid
Song:	Old MacDonald Had A Farm
Link:	https://youtu.be/tbywapBFO7Y
Lyrics:	Appendix 3, page 290

Old MacDonald Had A Farm (Thomas d'Urfey):

Old	Mac	Don	ald	had	a	farm	x
E	I	E	I	O	x	x	and
on	this	farm	he	had	a	cow	x
E	I	E	I	O			

LISTEN

YouTube Channel:	Nomi Yah
Playlist:	Writing Lyrics In A Grid
Song:	Bobby Shafto
Link:	https://youtu.be/ZmoSV0z9Rt4
Lyrics:	Appendix 3, page 286

Bobby Shafto (Traditional):

Bob	by	Shaf	to's	gone	to	sea	x
sil	ver	buck	les	on	his	knee	x
he'll	come	back	and	mar	ry	me	x
pret	ty	Bob	by	Shaf	x	to	x

LISTEN

YouTube Channel:	Nomi Yah
Playlist:	Writing Lyrics In A Grid
Song:	Yankee Doodle
Link:	https://youtu.be/-JoB5bCKsdY
Lyrics:	Appendix 3, page 298

Yankee Doodle (George M. Cohan):

Yan	kee	Doo	dle	went	to	town	x
<u>rid</u>	ing	on	a	po	x	ny	x
stuck	a	feath	er	in	his	hat	and
called	it	mac	a	ro	x	ni	x

<u>LISTEN</u>

YouTube Channel:	Nomi Yah
Playlist:	Writing Lyrics In A Grid
Song:	Angels We Have On High
Link:	https://youtu.be/WHWqj6gKS9g
Lyrics:	Appendix 3, page 285

Angels We Have Heard On High (James Chadwick):

an	gels	we	have	heard	<u>x on</u>	high	x
sweet	ly	sing	ing	o'er	<u>x the</u>	plains	x
and	the	moun	tains	in	<u>x re</u>	ply	x
ech	o	ing	their	joy	<u>x ous</u>	strain	x

The patterns in all these songs line up in an orderly way. Every downbeat has a syllable, with little or no syncopation.

If you're writing a song and want it to be easy to learn, with a classic feel, use the patterns of a lullaby. If you're going for an edgier style, do the opposite.

If you want your song to be both stimulating and memorable, use an artistic combination of predictable and unpredictable patterns.

EXERCISE

1. Write down the lyrics of a lullaby.

2. Begin at the top left box of the grid. Tap your finger in each box from left to right. Sing in time to your tapping. Begin at the top row and descend, always tapping left to right.

3. What box is your finger touching when you sing each syllable? Write that syllable into that box.

4. When all the lyrics are in the grid, identify patterns. Which lines match? Where are the rhymes? Does it look orderly and simple, like the lullabies in this chapter? Are there variations?

CHAPTER 5
WRITE A SONG IN A GRID

It would certainly be dull if all songs were lullabies or anthems. We'll move on to a modern genre, with more complex patterns. Try your hand at my original song Rows Of Roses. I'll let you in on the writing process and show you how writing lyrics on a grid helped me craft the words.

Rows Of Roses is one of my most popular songs. It has a charming story and a witty hook and those are two reasons why it's popular. But there's another subtler reason for its easy accessibility: craft. I spent a great deal of time on the technical crafting of these lyrics, using every technique I knew. Extensive hours of rewriting, combined with an compelling subject, resulted in what most people consider my best song.

I was inspired to write the song while sitting on my porch and looking at some rose bushes. The title popped into my mind Rows Of Roses and I knew right away it was a good hook. I thought about what kind of story could fit the title.

I came up with the storyline of a woman who starts out waiting on a man to bring her flowers, but later plants roses in her garden for herself. Although it was an anthem of female strength, I never felt like performing it. Rather than evoking a feeling of empowerment, the message conveyed the unpleasant emotion of isolation. I couldn't shake the feeling the story wasn't worthy of the hook, so I set the song aside.

When I finally returned to it, I threw out the whole song and made a fresh start. I went through several ideas until I eventually came up with a storyline that was as strong as the title. The new story was about grandpa planting a rose bush every anniversary for grandma. Most listeners think it's a true story about my family, which is a complement for a fiction writer.

Once I had a good hook and storyline, I worked on the sinker. I set out to rewrite the song dozens of times. Throughout the chapter, you'll see how I applied multiple techniques to achieve what appears to be a simple song.

LEARN THE SONG

Become familiar with the song by listening and reading the lyrics. Count from one to eight in time with the lyrics. After you know the song, we'll write it in a grid.

SONG
ROWS OF ROSES (Nomi Yah)

LINE NUMBERS
VERSE 1, LINE 1: When grandpa proposed, he gave her a rose
VERSE 1, LINE 2: On their wedding day, he gave a big bouquet
VERSE 1, LINE 3: On anniversaries, he went to nurseries
VERSE 1, LINE 4: Every year he chose a different color rose
VERSE 1, LINE 5: To put in the ground for her
VERSE 1, LINE 6: For fifty years
CHORUS, LINE 1 :She has rows of roses, growing in her garden
CHORUS, LINE 2: She has rows of roses, planted in her yard
CHORUS, LINE 3: She cuts and puts them in a vase
CHORUS, LINE 4: It puts a smile on her face
CHORUS, LINE 5: To see those rows and rows of roses
VERSE 2, LINE 1: As grandpa would say, a store-bought bouquet
VERSE 2, LINE 2: Doesn't last for long, now even though he's gone
VERSE 2, LINE 3: He still gives flowers to her
VERSE 2, LINE 4: For rest of her years

BRIDGE, LINE 1: We said come live with us, she wouldn't budge
BRIDGE, LINE 2: She decided to stay where she was
BRIDGE, LINE 3: Where she could breathe his undying love

LISTEN
YouTube Channel: Nomi Yah
Playlist: Writing Lyrics In A Grid
Song: Rows Of Roses
Link: https://youtu.be/7s4TDWMuDOY
Lyrics: Appendix 3, page 293

STEP 1

After familiarizing yourself with the song, begin deconstructing the verses. Start from the top, on the first line of the first verse. Write the line in the grid, then identify patterns.

Starting on the top left box of the grid, tap your finger inside each of the grid boxes, from left to right.

1	2	3	4	5	6	7	8

Repeat the eight taps across Row 1, finding the tempo of the song, and sing Verse 1, Line 1.

VERSE 1, LINE 1: When grandpa proposed, he gave her a rose

Your finger is tapping left to right, touching each of the eight boxes in Row 1, while you sing. What box is your finger touching on the first word "when"?

The first word "when" is not in Box 1 because it isn't on the downbeat. "When" is a pick-up note, before the downbeat.

Row 1, Box 8 = "when"

Verse 1, Line 1:

							when

Start over. Tap your finger from the top, from left to right, eight taps each row, singing Verse 1, Line 1 again. What box is your finger touching on the word "grandpa"? It starts on the downbeat, in Box 1.

Row 2, Box 1 = "grand"
Row 2, Box 2 = "x"
Row 2, Box 3 = "pa"

Verse 1, Line 1:

							when
grand	x	pa					

Start over from the top. What box is your finger touching on the word "proposed"?

Row 2, Box 4 = "pro"
Row 2, Box 5 = "posed"

Verse 1, Line 1:

							when
grand	x	pa	pro	posed			

Repeating the process, continue filling in the grid. What box is your finger touching on the next word "he"? The syllable "he" is in Row 2, Box 8 and that means Row 2, Boxes 6 and 7 are empty.

Row 2, Boxes 6 and 7 = "x"
Row 2, Box 8 = "he"

Verse 1, Line 1:

							when

grand	x	pa	pro	posed	x	x	he

What box is your finger touching on the word "gave"? "Gave" is on the downbeat.

Row 3, Box 1 = "gave"

Verse 1, Line 1:

							when
grand	x	pa	pro	posed	x	x	he
gave							

Row 3, Box 2 = "x"
Row 3, Box 3 = "her"

Verse 1, Line 1:

							when
grand	x	pa	pro	posed	x	x	he
gave	x	her					

Row 3, Box 4 = "a"

Verse 1, Line 1:

							when
grand	x	pa	pro	posed	x	x	he
gave	x	her	a				

Row 3, Box 5 = "rose"

Verse 1, Line 1:

							when
grand	x	pa	pro	posed	x	x	he
gave	x	her	a	rose			

Check your work. Go back to the top, from left to right, and tap your finger. Sing in time to the tapping rhythm. Make sure your finger is touching each syllable at the exact same time you sing it.

Verse 1, Line 1:

							when
grand	x	pa	pro	posed	x	x	he
gave	x	her	a	rose			

IDENTIFY PATTERNS

With Verse 1, Line 1 in the grid, we're able to analyze the patterns. Identify repetitions and variations appearing in the grid. Make note of anything of creative interest, such as rhyme or alliteration.

Verse 1, Line 1:

							when
grand	x	pa	pro	posed	x	x	he
gave	x	her	a	rose			

Rows 2 & 3, Boxes 1 have an alliteration "grandpa" and "gave".

Row 2, Boxes 3, 4 and 5 have an alliteration "pa", "pro" and "posed". The repetition of sound in alliteration has a subtle influence on the listener. Repetition makes a song more memorable because repetition is how we learn everything.

Boxes 5 are an internal rhyme "proposed" and "rose". Rhyming is the most well-known technique of songwriting. Rhyme uses repetition and variation at the same time. Part of a word repeats while another part changes. Internal rhymes add another opportunity to subtly influence a listener to remember the song and find it catchy.

STEP 2

We've analyzed Verse 1, Line 1, what's next? Go on to Verse 1, Line 2, right? Wait, think about the structure. We're looking for intentional repetition, not chronological order.

Listen to Verse 1 again and look for repetitions in the melody. You'll hear that Verse 1, Line 1 "when grandpa proposed, he gave her a rose" has the same melody as Verse 1, Line 3 "on anniversaries, he went to nurseries". There is melodic repetition in Lines 1 and 3.

Syllabalize Verse 1, Line 3 and compare the patterns to Line 1.

VERSE 1, LINE 3: On anniversaries, he went to nurseries

On a new grid, tap from left to right while singing. What box is your finger touching when you sing the word "on"?

"On" is the first word but is not in Box 1. It isn't on the downbeat, it's a pick-up note before the downbeat.

Row 1, Box 8 = "on"

Verse 1, Line 3:

							on

What box is your finger touching on the word "anniversaries"? The first syllable is in Row 2, Box 1, on the downbeat. The following syllables are on consecutive beats.

Row 2, Box 1 = "an"
Row 2, Box 2 = "ni"
Row 2, Box 3 = "ver"
Row 2, Box 4 = "sa"
Row 2, Box 5 = "ries"

Verse 1, Line 3:

							on
an	ni	ver	sa	ries			

Row 2, Boxes 6 and 7 = "x"
Row 2, Box 8 = "he"

Verse 1, Line 3:

							on
an	ni	ver	sa	ries	x	x	he

Row 3, Box 1 = "went"

Verse 1, Line 3:

							on
an	ni	ver	sa	ries	x	x	he
went							

Row 3, Box 2 = "to"

Verse 1, Line 3:

							on
an	ni	ver	sa	ries	x	x	he
went	to						

The syllables of "nurseries" are in Row 3, Boxes 3, 4 and 5.

Row 3, Box 3 = "nurs"
Row 3, Box 4 = "er"
Row 3, Box 5 = "ies"

Verse 1, Line 3:

							on
an	ni	ver	sa	ries	x	x	he

went	to	nurs	er	ies			

<u>IDENTIFY PATTERNS</u>

Verse 1, Line 3:

							on
an	ni	ver	sa	ries	x	x	he
went	to	nurs	er	ies			

Boxes 1 have a near alliteration "an" and "went".

Boxes 3, 4 and 5 are a triple-syllable rhyme "anniversaries" and "nurseries".

STEP 3

We've syllabalized and analyzed Verse 1, Lines 1 and 3 individually. Next compare the patterns in the two lines. The melody is the same in both lines, is the phrasing the same too?

Verse 1, Line 1:

							when
grand	x	pa	pro	posed	x	x	he
gave	x	her	a	rose			

Verse 1, Line 3:

							on
an	ni	ver	sa	ries	x	x	he
went	to	nurs	er	ies			

Rows 1 are identical.

Rows 2 are identical except Boxes 2. "Grandpa proposed" has four syllables and "anniversaries" has five syllables.

Rows 3 are identical except Boxes 2. "Gave her a rose" has four syllables and "went to nurseries" has five syllables.

Everything is the same on these two lines except in Boxes 2. Do I have to rewrite the lines to make them identical? No, I don't have to do anything, songwriting is art, not science. Syllabalizing is not a rule to construct every line with the same phrasing. It's a method of identifying patterns to clarify what is the same and what is different. It gives us precise knowledge for artistic choice, like putting on a pair of glasses and seeing a blur become a word. Syllabalizing uses our eyes to make music for our ears.

In Rows 2 and 3, Boxes 2, I'm deciding not to change the small variation. Too much repetition is boring and this adds a little interest without being distracting. Plus, I want to keep the triple-syllable rhyme "anniversaries" and "nurseries".

STEP 4

In the previous step, I allowed a variation between Verse 1, Lines 1 and 3 in Boxes 2. It makes me wonder: does Verse 2 have the same variation as Verse 1 or is it different?

Syllabalize musically, not chronologically. Instead of continuing to work on Verse 1, bounce over to Verse 2 and find out if the patterns match in Lines 1 and 3.

VERSE 2, LINE 1: As grandpa would say, a store-bought bouquet

Same as before, tap your finger in each box along Row 1, from left to right, while singing Verse 2, Line 1.

56

"As" is a pick-up note before the downbeat.

Row 1, Box 8 = "as"

Verse 2, Line 1:

							as

Row 2, Box 1 = "grand"
Row 2, Box 2 = "x"
Row 2, Box 3 = "pa"

Verse 2, Line 1:

							as
grand	x	pa					

Row 2, Box 4 = "would"

Verse 2, Line 1:

							as
grand	x	pa	would				

Row 2, Box 5 = "say"

Verse 2, Line 1:

							as
grand	x	pa	would	say			

Row 2, Boxes 6 and 7 = "x"
Row 2, Box 8 = "a"

Verse 2, Line 1:

							as
grand	x	pa	would	say	x	x	a

Row 3, Box 1 = "store"
Row 3, Box 2 = "x"
Row 3, Box 3 = "bought"

Verse 2, Line 1:

							as
grand	x	pa	would	say	x	x	a
store	x	bought					

Row 3, Box 4 = "bou"
Row 3, Box 5 = "quet"

Verse 2, Line 1:

							as
grand	x	pa	would	say	x	x	a
store	x	bought	bou	quet			

IDENTIFY PATTERNS

Verse 2, Line 1:

							as
grand	x	pa	would	say	x	x	a
store	x	bought	bou	quet			

Boxes 5 rhyme "say" and "bouquet".

Row 3, Boxes 3 and 4 start with an alliterative consonant "bought" and "bouquet".

STEP 5

We've syllabalized and analyzed Verse 1, Lines 1 and 3 and Verse 2, Line 1. Now compare patterns in the three lines. Verse

2 is only half a verse, as Verse 2, Lines 3 and 4 correspond musically to Verse 1, Lines 5 and 6.

Verse 1, Line 1:

							when
grand	x	pa	pro	posed	x	x	he
gave	x	her	a	rose			

Verse 1, Line 3:

							on
an	ni	ver	sa	ries	x	x	he
went	to	nurs	er	ies			

Verse 2, Line 1:

							as
grand	x	pa	would	say	x	x	a
store	x	bought	bou	quet			

Verse 1, Line 1 and Verse 2, Line 1 have identical patterns. Repetition in the beginning of each verse is strong writing. The first line of a verse is an important location, in terms of impact on a listener.

Verse 1, Line 3 has a variation in Boxes 2. I'll allow the variation because it subtly breaks up the repetition with a one-syllable variation. This adds interest and prevents monotony.

In both verses, Lines 1, we see that Rows 2, Boxes 1, 2 and 3 are literally identical, both having the word "grandpa" in the same place.

Rows 2 and 3 rhyme in all three lines in Boxes 5, "proposed" and "rose", "anniversaries" and "nurseries", "say" and "bouquet".

STEP 6

Having looked at the patterns in the verses for Lines 1 and 3, circle back to Lines 2. Starting on Verse 1, Line 2, syllabalize and identify patterns.

VERSE 1, LINE 2: On their wedding day, he gave a big bouquet

Tap your finger in the boxes, left to right, and place syllables in the grid as before.

"On" is on the downbeat.

Row 1, Box 1 = "on"

Verse 2, Line 2:

on							

"Their wedding" is syncopated, each syllable has only half a box. Underlined syllables "___" indicate there are two syllables in one box. This is also true when an empty space "x" and a syllable are in one box.

Row 1, Box 2 = "their" and "wed"
Row 1, Box 3 = "x" and "ding"

Verse 2, Line 2:

on	<u>their wed</u>	<u>x ding</u>					

Row 1, Box 4 = "day"

Verse 2, Line 2:

on	<u>their wed</u>	<u>x ding</u>	day				

Row 1, Boxes 5, 6 and 7 = "x"
Row 1, Box 8 = "he"

Verse 2, Line 2:

on	their wed	x ding	day	x	x	x	he

Row 2, Box 1 = "gave"

Verse 2, Line 2:

on	their wed	x ding	day	x	x	x	he
gave							

The next two syllables "a" and "big" are underlined to signify two syllables sharing one box.

Row 2, Box 2 = "a" and "big"

Verse 2, Line 2:

on	their wed	x ding	day	x	x	x	he
gave	a big						

Row 2, Box 3 = "x" and "bou"
Row 2, Box 4 = "quet"

Verse 2, Line 2:

on	their wed	x ding	day	x	x	x	he
gave	a big	x bou	quet				

IDENTIFY PATTERNS

Verse 2, Line 2:

on	their wed	x ding	day	x	x	x	he
gave	a big	x bou	quet				

Boxes 4 rhyme "day" and "bouquet".

In both rows, Boxes 1 and 4 are single syllable and Boxes 2 and 3 are double syllables.

STEP 7

Syncopated lyrics can be tricky to get right. It's hard to see exactly where to place a syncopated syllable in a crowded grid. It can be difficult to pinpoint precise phrasing when the boxes are cluttered. For syllabalizing to work correctly, it must be precise.

The simplest way to grid syncopated lyrics is to syllabalize in double-time. When there are multiple boxes with two syllables, patterns are easier to see in double-time since each syllable is given its own box. Slowing down provides more accuracy. Syllabalizing in double-time reveals the exact spot where the syncopated syllable lands.

Syllabalize in the same way as before. Tap your finger left to right and sing along. But in double-time, tap at a faster tempo and sing slower.

Count to eight on in this double-time grid.

1	x	2	x	3	x	4	x
5	x	6	x	7	x	8	x

Write Verse 1, Line 2 in the grid in double-time.

VERSE 1, LINE 2: On their wedding day, he gave a big bouquet

Row 1, Box 1 = "on"
Row 1, Box 2 = "x"
Row 1, Box 3 = "their"
Row 1, Box 4 = "wed"
Row 1, Box 5 = "x"
Row 1, Box 6 = "ding"
Row 1, Box 7 = "day"

Verse 1, Line 2 (double-time):

on	x	their	wed	x	ding	day	

The double syllables in one box are gone, making the patterns clearer to visualize. Continue syllabalizing in double-time.

Row 1, Box 8 = "x"
Row 2, Boxes 1 to 6 = "x"
Row 2, Box 7 = "he"

Verse 1, Line 2 (double-time):

on	x	their	wed	x	ding	day	x
x	x	x	x	x	x	he	

Row 2, Box 8 = "x"
Row 3, Box 1 = "gave"
Row 3, Box 2 = "x"
Row 3, Box 3 = "a"
Row 3, Box 4 = "big"
Row 3, Box 5 = "x"
Row 3, Box 6 = "bou"
Row 3, Box 7 = "quet"

Verse 1, Line 2 (double-time):

on	x	their	wed	x	ding	day	x
x	x	x	x	x	x	he	x
gave	x	a	big	x	bou	quet	

IDENTIFY PATTERNS

Verse 1, Line 2 (double-time):

on	x	their	wed	x	ding	day	x
x	x	x	x	x	x	he	x
gave	x	a	big	x	bou	quet	

In Rows 1 and 3, all the syllables and empty boxes match.

Rows 1 and 3, Boxes 7 rhyme "day" and "bouquet".

It's easier to recognize patterns of a syncopated line when using a double-time grid. Instead of squeezing two syllables in one box, in double-time each syllable has its own box.

The only variation between the phrase "on their wedding day" and "he gave a big bouquet" is the pick-up syllable "he" in Row 2, Box 7. I'll leave the variation because a pick-up syllable has less impact than one on a downbeat.

STEP 8

Verse 1, Line 2 is syllabalized. Next work on Verse 1, Line 4. You probably have the gist of syllabalizing by now, so we'll speed up a bit. Instead of gridding one syllable at a time, take on a whole line at once. If you get lost, go back and repeat the step. Make sure to understand each step before continuing on to the next.

VERSE 1, LINE 4: Every year he chose a different color rose

Row 1, Box 1 = "eve"
Row 1, Box 2 = "x"
Row 1, Box 3 = "ry"
Row 1, Box 4 = "year"
Row 1, Box 5 = "x"
Row 1, Box 6 = "he"
Row 1, Box 7 = "chose"

Verse 1, Line 4 (double-time):

eve	x	ry	year	x	he	chose	

Row 1, Box 8 = "x"
Row 2, Boxes 1 to 6 = "x"
Row 2, Box 7 = "a"

Verse 1, Line 4 (double-time):

eve	x	ry	year	x	he	chose	x

x	x	x	x	x	x	a	

Row 2, Box 8 = "x"
Row 3, Box 1 = "dif"
Row 3, Box 2 = "x"
Row 3, Box 3 = "ferent"
Row 3, Box 4 = "col"
Row 3, Box 5 = "x"
Row 3, Box 6 = "or"
Row 3, Box 7 = "rose"

Verse 1, Line 4 (double-time):

eve	x	ry	year	x	he	chose	x
x	x	x	x	x	x	a	x
dif	x	ferent	col	x	or	rose	

IDENTIFY PATTERNS

Verse 1, Line 4 (double-time):

eve	x	ry	year	x	he	chose	x
x	x	x	x	x	x	a	x
dif	x	ferent	col	x	or	rose	

The double-time grid reveals identical phrasing in Rows 1 and 3.

Rows 1 and 3, Boxes 7 rhyme "chose" and "rose".

All Rows, Boxes 2 and 5 are empty "x".

The phrasing of "every year he chose" and "a different color rose" are the same, except the pick-up syllable "a" in Row 2, Box 7.

STEP 9

In this step, compare Verse 1, Lines 2 and 4. Look for patterns of repetition and variation.

Verse 1, Line 2 (double-time):

on	x	their	wed	x	ding	day	x
x	x	x	x	x	x	he	x
gave	x	a	big	x	bou	quet	

Verse 1, Line 4 (double-time):

eve	x	ry	year	x	he	chose	x
x	x	x	x	x	x	a	x
dif	x	ferent	col	x	or	rose	

The syllables line up precisely the same in both lines.

Rows 2, Boxes 7 the pick-up syllable is the same in both lines "he" and "a". In previous steps, we called this a variation between the first and second parts of the phrases. But a repeated variation isn't really a variation.

In this example, the pick-up syllable "he" in Verse 1, Line 2 prevents the verse from being too repetitive, like a lullaby. But repeating the variation with the pick-up syllable "a" in Line 4 is a repetition that makes the song more memorable.

STEP 10

In Steps 1 through 5, we syllabalized Verse 1, Lines 1 and 3 and Verse 2, Line 1.

In Steps 6 through 9, we completed Verse 1, Lines 2 and 4.

What line should we work on next? If you said Verse 2, Line 2, you're getting the hang of it. We compare lines with the same melodic structure, although not necessarily even and odd.

Syllabalize in double-time by tapping faster and singing slower.

VERSE 2, LINE 2: Doesn't last for long, now even 'though he's gone

Row 1, Box 1 = "does"
Row 1, Box 2 = "x"
Row 1, Box 3 = "n't"
Row 1, Box 4 = "last"
Row 1, Box 5 = "x"
Row 1, Box 6 = "for"
Row 1, Box 7 = "long"

Verse 2, Line 2 (double-time):

does	x	n't	last	x	for	long	

Row 1, Box 8 = "x"
Row 2, Boxes 1, 2, 3, 4, 5 and 6 = "x"
Row 2, Box 7 = "now"

Verse 2, Line 2 (double-time):

does	x	n't	last	x	for	long	x
x	x	x	x	x	x	now	

Row 2, Box 8 = "x"
Row 3, Box 1 = "e"
Row 3, Box 2 = "x"
Row 3, Box 3 = "ven"
Row 3, Box 4 = "'though"
Row 3, Box 5 = "x"
Row 3, Box 6 = "he's"
Row 3, Box 7 = "gone"

Verse 2, Line 2 (double-time):

does	x	n't	last	x	for	long	x
x	x	x	x	x	x	now	x
e	x	ven	though	x	he's	gone	

IDENTIFY PATTERNS

Verse 2, Line 2 (double-time):

does	x	n't	last	x	for	long	x
x	x	x	x	x	x	now	x
e	x	ven	though	x	he's	gone	

Rows 1 and 3 are identical in phrasing.

Rows 1 and 3, Boxes 7 rhyme "long" and "gone".

The phrases "doesn't last for long" and "now even 'though he's gone" are the same, except the pick-up syllable "now" in Row 2, Box 7.

STEP 11

We syllabalized Verse 1, Lines 2 and 4 and Verse 2, Line 2. The next logical progression is to continue with the even lines and focus on Verse 2, Line 4. But while Verse 1 has four lines and a pre-chorus, Verse 2 only has two lines and a pre-chorus.

Most verses have the same number of lines, it's what the listener expects. I intentionally broke with tradition for reasons of prosody. Prosody is a subtle level of song craft that supports lyrical meaning with a corresponding musical counterpart. For example, prosody is when the notes of a melody go up at the same time the lyrics sing the word "up".

Prosody happens at Verse 2, Line 2, when the listener discovers Grandpa is no longer living. The jarring revelation matches the unexpected truncating of the verse.

Compare the even verse lines.

Verse 1, Line 2 (double-time):

on	x	their	wed	x	ding	day	x
x	x	x	x	x	x	he	x
gave	x	a	big	x	bou	quet	

Verse 1, Line 4 (double-time):

eve	x	ry	year	x	he	chose	x
x	x	x	x	x	x	a	x
dif	x	ferent	col	x	or	rose	

Verse 2, Line 2 (double-time):

does	x	n't	last	x	for	long	x
x	x	x	x	x	x	now	x
e	x	ven	though	x	he's	gone	

These lines have identical phrasing. The syllables and empty boxes are in the same exact places in all three.

All lines have a pickup syllable in Rows 2, Boxes 7 "he", "a", and "now".

Rhymes line up in Rows 1 and 3, Boxes 7, "day" and "bouquet", "chose" and "rose", "long" and "gone".

We saw in Step 5, Lines 1 and 3 of the verses have identical phrasing. Here we see Lines 2 and 4 are the same too. This is a traditional songwriting form, an old-fashioned style mirroring the old-fashioned grandparents in the story. The predictable repetitions add to the feeling the song is a classic. The steady patterns reflect the calm of living in one house for half a century.

This is prosody, where musical composition reflects lyrical content.

The only element upsetting the balance is the shortened Verse 2. This creates an unsettled feeling, as though something is wrong. It amplifies the emotional impact of the discovery that grandpa is gone. This is also prosody.

STEP 12

Lines 5 and 6 of the verses are a lift, a musical alert signaling the approaching chorus. A lift makes it easier to sing along with the chorus because the listener knows exactly when to come in.

This lift is mirrored by a rise in the melody, which begins low with "ground for her", goes up on "fifty years", and then soars highest at the hook "rows of roses". The melodic rise creates an emotional swell and primes the ear for an uplifting chorus.

I've added prosody by starting on a low tone with descending notes as the words sing "put in the ground for her". The melody echoes the physical activity of digging down into the dirt.

We'll work on the lifts from both verses in one step because they are almost identical.

VERSE 1, LINE 5: To put in the ground for her

Row 1, Box 4 = "to"
Row 1, Box 5 = "put"
Row 1, Box 6 = "x"
Row 1, Box 7 = "in"
Row 1, Box 8 = "the"
Row 2, Box 1 = "ground"
Row 2, Boxes 2, 3 and 4 = "x"
Row 2, Box 5 = "for"
Row 2, Boxes 6, 7 and 8 = "x"

Row 3, Box 1 = "her"

Verse 1, Line 5 (double-time):

			to	put	x	in	the
ground	x	x	x	for	x	x	x
her							

VERSE 1, LINE 6: For fifty years

Row 3, Boxes 2, 3, 4, 5 and 6 = "x"
Row 3, Box 7 = "for"
Row 3, Box 8 = "x"
Row 4, Box 1 = "fif"
Row 4, Boxes 2, 3 and 4 = "x"
Row 4, Box 5 = "ty"
Row 4, Boxes 6, 7 and 8 = "x"
Row 5, Box 1 = "years"

Verse 1, Line 5 & 6 (double-time):

			to	put	x	in	the
ground	x	x	x	for	x	x	x
her	x	x	x	x	x	for	x
fif	x	x	x	ty	x	x	x
years							

VERSE 2, LINE 5: He still gives flowers to her

Row 1, Box 4 = "he"
Row 1, Box 5 = "still"
Row 1, Box 6 = "x"
Row 1, Box 7 = "gives"
Row 1, Box 8 = "x"
Row 2, Box 1 = "flow"
Row 2, Box 2, 3 and 4 = "x"
Row 2, Box 5 = "ers"
Row 2, Box 6 and 7 = "x"
Row2, Box 8 = "to"

Row 3, Box 1 = "her"

Verse 2, Line 5 (double-time):

			he	still	x	gives	x
flow	x	x	x	ers	x	x	to
her							

VERSE 2, LINE 6: For the rest of her years

Row 3, Box 2, 3, 4, 5 and 6 = "x"
Row 3, Box 7 = "for"
Row 3, Box 8 = "the"
Row 4, Box 1 = "rest"
Row 4, Box 2, 3, 4 = "x"
Row 4, Box 5 = "of"
Row 4, Box 6 and 7 = "x"
Row 4, Box 8 = "her"
Row 5, Box 1 = "years"

Verse 2, Line 5 & 6 (double-time):

			he	still	x	gives	x
flow	x	x	x	ers	x	x	to
her	x	x	x	x	x	for	the
rest	x	x	x	of	x	x	her
years							

IDENTIFY PATTERNS

Verse 1, Line 5 & 6 (double-time):

			to	put	x	in	the
ground	x	x	x	for	x	x	x
her	x	x	x	x	x	for	x
fif	x	x	x	ty	x	x	x
years							

Verse 2, Line 5 & 6 (double-time):

			he	still	x	gives	x
flow	x	x	x	ers	x	x	to
her	x	x	x	x	x	for	the
rest	x	x	x	of	x	x	her
years							

Rows 1 are the same except Boxes 8, with Verse 1 having an extra syllable "the".

Rows 2 are the same except Boxes 8, with Verse 2 having an extra syllable "to".

Rows 3 are the same except Boxes 8, with Verse 2 having an extra syllable "the".

Rows 4 are the same except Boxes 8, with Verse 2 having an extra syllable "her".

Rows 5 are the same.

The only variations are in Boxes 8. I'm in favor of deleting unnecessary words, but the conversational sentence structures work well and the variations are all in the same place. So, I'm not going to rewrite Boxes 8.

Rows 3 and 5, Boxes 1 have the same near rhyme in both verses "her" and "years". This repetition helps to counter-balance the variations in Boxes 8.

Much of the craft of songwriting is the use of repetition and variation. Syllabalizing is a method of becoming acutely aware of which syllables are phrased the same and which are different. If you feel like you have too much variation, you can pinpoint which syllables need to change. If there's too much repetition, you can identify the parts to rewrite.

Is it getting clearer? With practice, the technique of writing lyrics in a grid will be internalized and you'll utilize the tool frequently.

STEP 13

Put all the verse lines together and look for additional patterns. You'll see an interesting perspective on song structure.

Put the grids side by side to make it easier to compare patterns.

Verse 1 (double-time):

						when	x
grand	x	x	x	pa	x	pro	x
posed	x	x	x	x	x	he	x
gave	x	x	x	her	x	a	x
rose	x	x	x	x	x	x	x
on	x	their	wed	x	ding	day	x
x	x	x	x	x	x	he	x
gave	x	a	big	x	bou	quet	x
x	x	x	x	x	x	on	x
an	x	ni	ver	x	x	sa	x
ries	x	x	x	x	x	he	x
went	x	to	nurs	x	x	er	x
ies	x	x	x	x	x	x	x
eve	x	ry	year	x	he	chose	x
x	x	x	x	x	x	a	x
dif	x	ferent	col	x	lor	rose	x
x	x	x	to	put	x	in	the
ground	x	x	x	for	x	x	x
her	x	x	x	x	x	for	x
fif	x	x	x	ty	x	x	x
years							

Verse 2 (double-time):

						as	x
grand	x	x	x	pa	x	would	x
say	x	x	x	x	x	a	x
store	x	x	x	bought	x	bou	x
quet	x	x	x	x	x	x	x
does	x	n't	last	x	for	long	x
x	x	x	x	x	x	now	x
e	x	ven	though	x	he's	gone	x
x	x	x	he	still	x	gives	x
flow	x	x	x	ers	x	x	to
her	x	x	x	x	x	for	the
rest	x	x	x	of	x	x	her
years							

The phrasing in these verses is identical, except in the lifts, where there are variations in Boxes 8.

Consistent phrasing makes the song feel classic. The layers are complex, but it sounds simple because of sparing use of variation.

Don't spend too much time analyzing a whole verse or an entire song. Syllabalizing works best for microscopic inspection. But it can be interesting to look at overall patterns.

STEP 14

A chorus holds a song together. The verses tell the story and the chorus sums up the meaning, culminating in the title or hook. A hook becomes memorable by repetition. For a chorus to be catchy, it has to be easy and enjoyable to sing. Syllabalizing is a fundamental tool to achieve this.

Listen to the chorus again and find repetitions in the melody. You'll notice right away, the first part of Chorus, Line 1 "rows of roses" is identical in words and melody to the first part of Chorus, Line 2. Since the first parts of the lines are the same, next see how the second parts compare.

Tap your finger in each box along Row 1, from left to right, in double-time. Sing Chorus, Line 1 and fill in the syllables in the corresponding boxes.

CHORUS, LINE 1: She has rows of roses, growing in her garden

Row 1, Box 5 = "she"
Row 1, Box 6 = "x"
Row 1, Box 7 = "has"
Row 1, Box 8 = "x"
Row 2, Box 1 = "rows"
Row 2, Boxes 2, 3, 4, 5 and 6 = "x"
Row 2, Box 7 = "of"
Row 2, Box 8 = "x"
Row 3, Box 5 = "ros"
Row 3, Boxes 2, 3 and 4 = "x"
Row 3, Box 5 = "es"

Chorus, Line 1 (double-time):

				she	x	has	x
rows	x	x	x	x	x	of	x
ros	x	x	x	es			

Row 3, Boxes 6, 7 and 8 = "x"
Row 4, Boxes 1 and 2 = "x"
Row 4, Box 3 = "grow"
Row 4, Box 4 = "ing"
Row 4, Box 5 = "in"
Row 4, Box 6 = "her"
Row 4, Boxes 7 and 8 = "x"
Row 5, Box 1 = "gar"
Row 5, Box 2 = "x"

Row 5, Box 3 = "den"

Chorus, Line 1 (double-time):

				she	x	has	x
rows	x	x	x	x	x	of	x
ros	x	x	x	es	x	x	x
x	x	grow	ing	in	her	x	x
gar	x	den					

IDENTIFY PATTERNS

Chorus, Line 1 (double-time):

				she	x	has	x
rows	x	x	x	x	x	of	x
ros	x	x	x	es	x	x	x
x	x	grow	ing	in	her	x	x
gar	x	den					

Row 2, Box 1, the first syllable of the title hook "rows" lands on the downbeat. This is a strong beginning for a chorus since it emphasizes the hook.

Row 3, Box 1 is the same syllable as Row 2, Box 1, although it has a different meaning. Using a homonym on a hook is a clever technique. It adds to the strength of the hook by making a repetitive sound.

STEP 15

Chorus, Line 2 is almost the same as Line 1. The first half is identical and can be copied.

CHORUS, LINE 2: She has rows of roses, planted in her yard

Row 1, Box 5 = "she"
Row 1, Box 6 = "x"
Row 1, Box 7 = "has"
Row 1, Box 8 = "x"
Row 2, Box 1 = "rows"
Row 2, Boxes 2, 3, 4, 5 and 6 = "x"
Row 2, Box 7 = "of"
Row 2, Box 8 = "x"
Row 3, Box 5 = "ros"
Row 3, Boxes 2, 3 and 4 = "x"
Row 3, Box 5 = "es"

Chorus, Line 2 (double-time):

				she	x	has	x
rows	x	x	x	x	x	of	x
ros	x	x	x	es			

Row 3, Boxes 6, 7 and 8 = "x"
Row 4, Boxes 1 and 2 = "x"
Row 4, Box 3 = "plant"
Row 4, Box 4 = "ed"
Row 4, Box 5 = "in"
Row 4, Box 6 = "her"
Row 4, Boxes 7 and 8 = "x"
Row 5, Box 1 = "yard"

Chorus, Line 2 (double-time):

				she	x	has	x
rows	x	x	x	x	x	of	x
ros	x	x	x	es	x	x	x
x	x	plant	ed	in	her	x	x
yard							

IDENTIFY PATTERNS

Are Chorus, Lines 1 and 2 the same? Are they different? Compare the patterns.

Chorus, Line 1 (double-time):

				she	x	has	x
rows	x	x	x	x	x	of	x
ros	x	x	x	es	x	x	x
x	x	grow	ing	in	her	x	x
gar	x	den					

Chorus, Line 2 (double-time):

				she	x	has	x
rows	x	x	x	x	x	of	x
ros	x	x	x	es	x	x	x
x	x	plant	ed	in	her	x	x
yard							

Rows 1, 2 and 3 have identical patterns and words.

Rows 4 have the same pattern and different words.

Rows 5, Boxes 1 rhyme "garden" in Line 1 and "yard" in Line 2.

Rows 5, Boxes 2 are empty "x".

Rows 5, Boxes 3 are different, with Line 1 having two syllables "garden" and Line 2 having one syllable "yard".

STEP 16

Chorus, Line 1 (double-time):

				she	x	has	x
rows	x	x	x	x	x	of	x

ros	x	x	x	es	x	x	x
x	x	grow	ing	in	her	x	x
gar	x	den					

Chorus, Line 2 (double-time):

				she	x	has	x
rows	x	x	x	x	x	of	x
ros	x	x	x	es	x	x	x
x	x	plant	ed	in	her	x	x
yard							

Rows 5, Boxes 3 are different, with Line 1 having an extra syllable. Too many variations in a chorus weakens it, making it harder for a listener to learn and remember. How can I rewrite it and take out the variation?

I try matching Chorus, Lines 1 and 2 by switching it around and rhyming "yard" with "hard", a more consistent one-syllable rhyme. My rewrite is "she has rows of roses planted in her yard / she has rows of roses when her life is hard / she cuts and puts them in a vase / it puts her in a better place." It's a good try, but I don't like the new version. "When her life is hard" has a storyline that isn't explained. "Puts her in a better place" is a dated saying. This draft belongs in the reject pile.

I'm leaving Rows 5 the way I first wrote it for the time being. Go on and write the next line in the grid to see if the extra syllable in "garden" can stay or if the line still needs rewriting.

STEP 17

Make sure the previous line Chorus, Line 2 "growing in her garden" fits with the following Line 3. Start by putting Chorus, Line 3 in the grid.

CHORUS, LINE 3: She cuts and puts them in a vase
Row 1, Box 3 = "she"
Row 1, Box 4 = "x"
Row 1, Box 5 = "cuts"
Row 1, Box 6 = "x"
Row 1, Box 7 = "and"
Row 1, Box 8 = "x"
Row 2, Box 1 = "puts"
Row 2, Box 2 = "x"
Row 2, Box 3 = "them"
Row 2, Box 4 = "in"
Row 2, Box 5 = "x"
Row 2, Box 6 = "a"
Row 2, Box 7 = "x"
Row 2, Box 8 = "vase"

Chorus, Line 3 (double-time):

		She	x	cuts	x	and	x
puts	x	them	in	x	a	x	vase

IDENTIFY PATTERNS

Chorus, Line 3 (double-time):

		she	x	cuts	x	and	x
puts	x	them	in	x	a	x	vase

Row 1, Box 5 and Row 2, Box 1 are internal near rhymes "cuts" and "puts"

Chorus Line 3 is very syncopated.

STEP 18

In Step 15, there was one more syllable in Chorus, Line 1 "garden" than in Chorus, Line 2 "yard". Is the variation is going to work? Put Chorus, Lines 1, 2 and 3 all in one grid and see how they fit together.

Chorus, Lines 1, 2 & 3 (double-time):

				she	x	has	x
rows	x	x	x	x	x	of	x
ros	x	x	x	es	x	x	x
x	x	grow	ing	in	her	x	x
gar	x	den	x	she	x	has	x
rows	x	x	x	x	x	of	x
ros	x	x	x	es	x	x	x
x	x	plant	ed	in	her	x	x
yard	x	she	x	cuts	x	and	x
puts	x	them	in	x	a	x	vase

When we compared the lines in separate grids, we saw a variation. Chorus, Line 1 "garden" has one more syllable than Chorus, Line 2 "yard". But look at it together with the following line and we see a pattern of identical phrasing. Row 5 "garden she has" is four syllables and so is Row 9 "yard she cuts and".

What appeared to be a variation at first, turned out not to be. The end of each line has exactly enough space for the pick-up of the following line.

STEP 19

Chorus, Lines 1 and 2 are repetitive. Chorus, Line 3 is completely different.

Are Chorus, Lines 3 and 4 the same or different? Syllabalize Line 4 and then compare the lines.

CHORUS, LINE 4: It puts a smile on her face
Although "smile" is technically one syllable, it's pronounced as two syllables "sma" and "yul". Use the symbol dash "-" to signify the second syllable.

Row 1, Box 3 = "it"
Row 1, Box 4 = "x"
Row 1, Box 5 = "puts"
Row 1, Box 6 = "x"
Row 1, Box 7 = "a"
Row 1, Box 8 = "x"
Row 2, Box 1 = "smile"
Row 2, Box 2 = "x"
Row 2, Box 3 = "-"

Chorus, Line 4 (double-time):

		it	x	puts	x	a	x
smile	x	-	on	x	her	x	face

IDENTIFY PATTERNS

Chorus, Line 3 (double-time):

		she	x	cuts	x	and	x
puts	x	them	in	x	a	x	vase

Chorus, Line 4 (double-time):

		it	x	puts	x	a	x
smile	x	-	on	x	her	x	face

Rows 1, Boxes 5 have an internal near rhyme "cuts" and "puts". Rows 2, Boxes 4 rhyme "vase" and "face". I like using strong vowels, like the hard "a", in a chorus.

Chorus, Lines 3 and 4 have identical syncopated patterns. It's risky to put so many syncopated lyrics in a chorus because it can be difficult for a listener to sing along. I solved the issue by repeating the tricky part twice in a row, making it easier to learn.

STEP 20

In this step, continue on to the final line of the chorus. Syllabalize and identify patterns in Chorus, Line 5.

CHORUS, LINE 5: To see those rows and rows of roses

Row 1, Box 3 = "to"
Row 1, Box 4 = "x"
Row 1, Box 5 = "see"
Row 1, Box 6 = "x"
Row 1, Box 7 = "those"
Row 1, Box 8 = "x"
Row 2, Box 1 = "rows"

Chorus, Line 5 (double-time):

		to	x	see	x	those	x
rows							

Row 2, Box 2, 3, 4, 5 and 6 = "x"
Row 2, Box 7 = "and"
Row 2, Box 8 = "x"
Row 3, Box 1 = "rows"

Chorus, Line 5 (double-time):

		to	x	see	x	those	x
rows	x	x	x	x	x	and	x
rows							

Row 3, Box 2, 3, 4, 5 and 6 = "x"
Row 3, Box 7 = "of"

Row 3, Box 8 = "x"
Row 4, Box 1 = "ros"
Row 4, Box 2 = "x"
Row 4, Box 3 = "es"

Chorus, Line 5 (double-time):

		to	x	see	x	those	x
rows	x	x	x	x	x	and	x
rows	x	x	x	x	x	of	x
ros	x	x	x	es			

IDENTIFY PATTERNS

Chorus, Line 5 (double-time):

		to	x	see	x	those	x
rows	x	x	x	x	x	and	x
rows	x	x	x	x	x	of	x
ros	x	x	x	es			

Rows 2 and 3, Boxes 1, 2, 3, 4, 5 and 6 are identical. The repetition is on the hook and it lands on the downbeats. These elements make the hook catchier.

Row 1, Box 7 "those" is an internal rhyme with Rows 2 and 3, Boxes 1 "rows". At first, I wrote "the rows", but then I thought of "those rows". Rhyming the hook is a wonderful technique to strengthen the chorus.

STEP 21

IDENTIFY PATTERNS

Chorus (double-time):

				she	x	has	x
rows	x	x	x	x	x	of	x

ros	x	x	x	es	x	x	x
x	x	grow	ing	in	her	x	x
gar	x	den	x	she	x	has	x
rows	x	x	x	x	x	of	x
ros	x	x	x	es	x	x	x
x	x	plant	ed	in	her	x	x
yard	x	she	x	cuts	x	and	x
puts	x	them	in	x	a	x	vase
x	x	it	x	puts	x	a	x
smi	x	le	on	x	her	x	face
x	x	to	x	see	x	those	x
rows	x	x	x	x	x	and	x
rows	x	x	x	x	x	of	x
ros	x	x	x	es			

In Rows 2, 3, 6, 7, 14, 15 and 16, there's a pattern of empty boxes. The other rows have short syncopated syllables. The pattern alternates between sparse and dense, adding movement to the chorus.

The hook syllable, whether "rows" or "rose", always lands in the same place, on the downbeat. This adds to making the chorus more memorable. The hook is pounded into the listener's brain, using precise repetition and no variation, like a children's lullaby.

STEP 22

All that remains to syllabalize is the bridge. It's a short section, so we can tackle the whole thing at once. These lines are mostly syncopated, so we'll continue to syllabalize in double-time to make it easier to identify patterns.

BRIDGE, LINE 1: We said come live with us, she wouldn't budge

Row 1, Box 3 = "we"
Row 1, Box 4 = "said"
Row 1, Box 5 = "come"
Row 1, Box 6 = "live"
Row 1, Box 7 = "with"
Row 1, Box 8 = "us"

Bridge (double-time):

		we	said	come	live	with	us

Row 2, Boxes 1 and 2 = "x"
Row 2, Box 3 = "she"
Row 2, Box 4 = "would"
Row 2, Boxes 5 and 6 = "x"
Row 2, Box 7 = "n't"
Row 2, Box 8 = "budge"

Bridge (double-time):

		we	said	come	live	with	us
x	x	she	would	x	x	n't	budge

BRIDGE, LINE 2: She decided to stay where she was
Rows 3 and 4 = "x"

Bridge (double-time):

		we	said	come	live	with	us
x	x	she	would	x	x	n't	budge
x	x	x	x	x	x	x	x
x	x	x	x	x	x	x	x

Row 5, Boxes 1 and 2 = "x"
Row 5, Box 3 = "she"
Row 5, Box 4 = "de"
Row 5, Box 5 = "cid"
Row 5, Box 6 = "ed"
Row 5, Box 7 = "to"
Row 5, Box 8 = "stay"

Bridge (double-time):

		we	said	come	live	with	us
x	x	she	would	x	x	n't	budge
x	x	x	x	x	x	x	x
x	x	x	x	x	x	x	x
x	x	she	de	cid	ed	to	stay

Row 6, Boxes 1, 2, 3 and 4 = "x"
Row 6, Box 5 = "where"
Row 6, Box 6 = "x"
Row 6, Box 7 = "she"
Row 6, Box 8 = "was"

Bridge (double-time):

		we	said	come	live	with	us
x	x	she	would	x	x	n't	budge
x	x	x	x	x	x	x	x
x	x	x	x	x	x	x	x
x	x	she	de	cid	ed	to	stay
x	x	x	x	where	x	she	was

BRIDGE, LINE 3: Where she could breathe his undying love

Rows 7 and 8 = "x"

Bridge (double-time):

		we	said	come	live	with	us
x	x	she	would	x	x	n't	budge
x	x	x	x	x	x	x	x
x	x	x	x	x	x	x	x
x	x	she	de	cid	ed	to	stay
x	x	x	x	where	x	she	was
x	x	x	x	x	x	x	x
x	x	x	x	x	x	x	x

Row 9, Boxes 1, 2, 3 and 4 = "x"
Row 9, Box 5 = "where"
Row 9, Box 6 = "she"
Row 9, Box 7 = "could"
Row 9, Box 8 = "breathe"
Row 10, Boxes 1 and 2 = "x"
Row 10, Box 3 = "his"
Row 10, Box 4 = "x"
Row 10, Box 5 = "un"
Row 10, Box 6 = "dy"
Row 10, Box 7 = "ing"
Row 10, Box 8 = "love"

Bridge (double-time):

		we	said	come	live	with	us
x	x	she	would	x	x	n't	budge
x	x	x	x	x	x	x	x
x	x	x	x	x	x	x	x
x	x	she	de	cid	ed	to	stay
x	x	x	x	where	x	she	was
x	x	x	x	x	x	x	x
x	x	x	x	x	x	x	x
x	x	x	x	where	she	could	breathe
x	x	his	x	un	dy	ing	love

BRIDGE, LINE 4: His undying love

Row 11, Boxes 1 and 2 = "x"
Row 11, Box 3 = "his"
Row 11, Box 4 = "x"
Row 11, Box 5 = "un"
Row 11, Box 6 = "dy"
Row 11, Box 7 = "ing"
Row 11, Box 8 = "love"

Bridge (double-time):

		we	said	come	live	with	us
X	X	she	would	X	X	n't	budge
X	X	X	X	X	X	X	X
X	X	X	X	X	X	X	X
X	X	she	de	cid	ed	to	stay
X	X	X	X	where	X	she	was
X	X	X	X	X	X	X	X
X	X	X	X	X	X	X	X
X	X	X	X	where	she	could	breathe
X	X	his	X	un	dy	ing	love
X	X	his	X	un	dy	ing	love

IDENTIFY PATTERNS

Bridge (double-time):

		we	said	come	live	with	us
X	X	she	would	X	X	n't	budge
X	X	X	X	X	X	X	X
X	X	X	X	X	X	X	X
X	X	she	de	cid	ed	to	stay
X	X	X	X	where	X	she	was
X	X	X	X	X	X	X	X
X	X	X	X	X	X	X	X
X	X	X	X	where	she	could	breathe
X	X	his	X	un	dy	ing	love
X	X	his	X	un	dy	ing	love

All Rows, Boxes 1 and 2 are empty. Rows 3, 4, 7 and 8 are completely empty. There's a lot of space in the bridge, making it very different than the rest of the song. The rows of space provide a high contrast to the syncopated rows. The contrast adds extra drama, a good thing in a bridge.

90

Row 2, Box 8 "budge" is a near rhyme to Row 6, Box 8 "was" and Rows 10 and 11, Boxes 8 "love".

Rows 1 and 5 have the same phrasing.
Rows 10 and 11 are exactly the same.

The rest of the bridge has a lot of variation. I welcome differences more in the bridge than in the rest of the song. A bridge is a departure, with the function of adding variation to provide interest late in the song.

When the complex bridge returns to the simplicity of the chorus, it feels like a relief. The release carries the satisfied listener to the end of the song.

SUMMARY

In Chapter 5, you learned how to:
- Syllabalize in double-time
- Use prosody to add depth to the story
- Rhyme the hook to strengthen the chorus
- Use a lift as a musical alert that the chorus is approaching

We syllabalized the song in twenty-two steps. It sounds like a lot, but it was really just two actions, repeated as needed. Breaking it up into granular steps makes it easier to learn, but in practice it's only these two actions:
1. Write lyrics in a grid
2. Look at patterns

Much of the time, I don't syllabalize an entire song. Mostly I use the method to fix lyrical problems with surgical precision. But in this example, since we syllabalized the song from beginning to end, we may as well put it all together. It can be interesting to view the words as a whole in a grid. You can see overall patterns as you visualize lyrics in a fresh way.

It looks odd, we're used to seeing lyrics laid out in stanzas, like poetry. But this is a closer representation of how we actually hear a song. It's a map of all the phrasing laid out in a grid.

Rows Of Roses (double-time):

						when	x
grand	x	x	x	pa	x	pro	x
posed	x	x	x	x	x	he	x
gave	x	x	x	her	x	a	x
rose	x	x	x	x	x	x	x
on	x	their	wed	x	ding	day	x
x	x	x	x	x	x	he	x
gave	x	a	big	x	bou	quet	x
x	x	x	x	x	x	on	x
an	x	ni	ver	x	x	sa	x
ries	x	x	x	x	x	he	x
went	x	to	nurs	x	x	er	x
ies	x	x	x	x	x	x	x
eve	x	ry	year	x	he	chose	x
x	x	x	x	x	x	a	x
dif	x	ferent	col	x	lor	rose	x
x	x	x	to	put	x	in	the
ground	x	x	x	for	x	x	x
her	x	x	x	x	x	for	x
fif	x	x	x	ty	x	x	x
years	x	x	x	she	x	has	x
rows	x	x	x	x	x	of	x
ros	x	x	x	es	x	x	x
x	x	grow	ing	in	her	x	x
gar	x	den	x	she	x	has	x
rows	x	x	x	x	x	of	x
ros	x	x	x	es	x	x	x
x	x	plant	ed	in	her	x	x
yard	x	she	x	cuts	x	and	x
puts	x	them	in	x	a	x	vase
x	x	it	x	puts	x	a	x
smile	x	-	on	x	her	x	face

x	x	to	x	see	x	those	x
rows	x	x	x	x	x	and	x
rows	x	x	x	x	x	of	x
ros	x	x	x	es	x	x	x
x	x	x	x	x	x	as	x
grand	x	x	x	pa	x	would	x
say	x	x	x	x	x	a	x
store	x	x	x	bought	x	bou	x
quet	x	x	x	x	x	x	x
does	x	n't	last	x	for	long	x
x	x	x	x	x	x	now	x
e	x	ven	though	x	he's	gone	x
x	x	x	he	still	x	gives	x
flow	x	x	x	ers	x	x	to
her	x	x	x	x	x	for	the
rest	x	x	x	of	x	x	her
years	x	x	x	she	x	has	x
rows	x	x	x	x	x	of	x
ros	x	x	x	es	x	x	x
x	x	grow	ing	in	her	x	x
gar	x	den	x	she	x	has	x
rows	x	x	x	x	x	of	x
ros	x	x	x	es	x	x	x
x	x	plant	ed	in	her	x	x
yard	x	she	x	cuts	x	and	x
puts	x	them	in	x	a	x	vase
x	x	it	x	puts	x	a	x
smile	x	-	on	x	her	x	face
x	x	to	x	see	x	those	x
rows	x	x	x	x	x	and	x
rows	x	x	x	x	x	of	x
ros	x	x	x	es	x	x	x
x	x	we	said	come	live	with	us
x	x	she	would	x	x	n't	budge
x	x	x	x	x	x	x	x
x	x	x	x	x	x	x	x
x	x	she	de	cid	ed	to	stay

x	x	x	x	where	x	she	was
x	x	x	x	x	x	x	x
x	x	x	x	x	x	x	x
x	x	x	x	where	she	could	breathe
x	x	his	x	un	dy	ing	love
x	x	his	x	un	dy	ing	love
x	x	x	x	x	x	x	x
rows	x	x	x	x	x	of	x
ros	x	x	x	es	x	x	x
x	x	grow	ing	in	her	x	x
gar	x	den	x	she	x	has	x
rows	x	x	x	x	x	of	x
ros	x	x	x	es	x	x	x
x	x	plant	ed	in	her	x	x
yard	x	she	x	cuts	x	and	x
puts	x	them	in	x	a	x	vase
x	x	it	x	puts	x	a	x
smile	x	-	on	x	her	x	face
x	x	to	x	see	x	those	x
rows	x	x	x	x	x	and	x
rows	x	x	x	x	x	of	x
ros	x	x	x	es			

It's interesting to look at an entire song in a grid. But we're not going to analyze patterns at this macro level. We've already discussed each individual section in depth.

Writing lyrics in a grid is an easy technique to use and the learning curve is small. But unfortunately, it's dry and methodical to explain. So, if you're still with me, congratulations, you're obsessed with pursuing greatness.

EXERCISE

1. Write down the lyrics of a song.

2. Tap your finger, from left to right, and sing in time. If many boxes contain more than one syllable, change to double-time.

3. What box is your finger touching when you sing each syllable? Write that syllable into that box.

4. When all the lyrics are in the grid, identify patterns. Which lines match? Do the verses match? Is the chorus similar or different from the verse pattern? Where are the rhymes?

CHAPTER 6
WRITE ANOTHER SONG IN A GRID

We'll solidify the concepts we've been discussing by practicing on another example. This is a song I wrote called Perfect Enough.

A friend inspired the story. He was always running at full-speed but was always late. He was a very successful person and was driven by extravagant taste. But in my opinion, he was doing too much and missing out on what really mattered. He was chasing a lifestyle that generated stress and unhappiness.

My friend overvalued possessions and undervalued time with his loved ones. The lyrics of Perfect Enough give advice to pay less attention to materialism and focus more on family.

LEARN THE SONG

Become familiar with the song by listening and reading the lyrics. Count to eight in time with the lyrics. After you know the song, we'll syllabalize it.

The verses are numbered with five lines, but the fifth line is really a tag on the fourth. It's in a separate line to make it easier to compare patterns. The tag is part of the song form, not a variation, because it is repeated in every verse.

SONG
PERFECT ENOUGH (Nomi Yah)

<u>**LINE NUMBERS**</u>
VERSE 1, LINE 1: Your child gets tall, while you are busy
VERSE 1, LINE 2: Think of it, isn't it really a shame
VERSE 1, LINE 3: If you're missing it all, childhood is brief
VERSE 1, LINE 4: Picture books and loose teeth and that Little League game
VERSE 1, LINE 5: Man, relax
CHORUS, LINE 1: Life is perfect enough
CHORUS, LINE 2: Perfect enough, Lord
CHORUS, LINE 3: It could be better, sometimes it's rough
CHORUS, LINE 4: But today is perfect enough
VERSE 2, LINE 1: Your Jaguar's fast, but you're running late
VERSE 2, LINE 2: You won't catch the plane, but you'll get on the next
VERSE 2, LINE 3: And you'll fly first-class, trying to achieve
VERSE 2, LINE 4: The American Dream, while you're piling up debts
VERSE 2, LINE 5: Man, relax
BRIDGE, LINE 1: You should be proud of what you've done
BRIDGE, LINE 2: Look how far you've come
VERSE 3, LINE 1: It's all a matter of priority, keep up what you're doing
VERSE 3, LINE 2: If it doesn't ruin the time that you spend
VERSE 3, LINE 3: With your family, you are their rock
VERSE 3, LINE 4: And they love when you walk through that door at the end
VERSE 3, LINE 5: Of the day

<u>**LISTEN**</u>
YouTube Channel: Nomi Yah
Playlist: Writing Lyrics In A Grid
Song: Perfect Enough
Link: https://youtu.be/mWqGMUoNB1g
Lyrics: Appendix 3, page 291

STEP I

Listen to the verse and find repeating melodies. This song, like many, has one melody in the odd lines and another melody in the even lines. See if the odd lines in Verse 1, Lines 1 and 3, are a match. Don't include Line 5 because the melody is different on the tag.

It's useful to syllabalize lines grouped together based on similarity of melody. The goal of writing lyrics in a grid is to make words follow a melody tightly, scrutinizing variations. This goes back to the basics, repetition makes a song easier to remember, while variation makes it more interesting.

In the previous chapter, we used double-time grids to handle syncopated lyrics. In this song, we'll do the same.

VERSE 1, LINE 1: Your child gets tall, while you are busy

Reading the word "child", it looks like it has one syllable. But it's pronounced with two syllables "cha" and "yald". Use the dash symbol "-" to indicate the second syllable.

Row 1, Box 8 = "your"
Row 2, Box 1 = "child"
Row 2, Box 2 = "-"
Row 2, Box 3 = "gets"
Row 2, Box 4 = "x"
Row 2, Box 5 = "tall"
Row 2, Boxes 6, 7 and 8 = "x"
Row 3, Box 1 = "while"
Row 3, Box 2 = "you"
Row 3, Box 3 = "are"
Row 3, Box 4 = "bus"
Row 3, Box 5 = "x"
Row 3, Box 6 = "y"

Verse 1, Line 1 (double-time):

							your
child	-	gets	x	tall	x	x	x
while	you	are	bus	x	y		

VERSE 1, LINE 3: If you're missing it all, childhood is brief

Although "child" is pronounced with two syllables, when it's in the word "childhood" it has one syllable.

Row 1, Box 6 = "if"
Row 1, Box 7 = "x"
Row 1, Box 8 = "you're"
Row 2, Box 1 = "miss"
Row 2, Box 2 = "ing"
Row 2, Box 3 = "it"
Row 2, Box 4 = "x"
Row 2, Box 5 = "all"
Row 2, Box 6, 7 and 8 = "x"
Row 3, Box 1 = "child"
Row 3, Box 2 = "hood"
Row 3, Box 3 = "is"
Row 3, Box 4 = "brief"

Verse 1, Line 3 (double-time):

					if	x	you're
miss	ing	it	x	all	x	x	x
child	hood	is	brief				

IDENTIFY PATTERNS

Verse 1, Line 1 (double-time):

							your
child	-	gets	x	tall	x	x	x
while	you	are	bus	x	y		

Verse 1, Line 3 (double-time):

					if	x	you're
miss	ing	it	x	all	x	x	x
child	hood	is	brief				

Rows 1, Boxes 6 are different, Verse 1, Line 3 has an extra syllable "if".

Rows 2 have identical phrasing.

Rows 2, Boxes 5 rhyme "tall" and "all".
Rows 3, Boxes 1 rhyme "while" and "child".

Rows 3, Boxes 4 have alliteration "busy" and "brief".

Rows 3, Boxes 6 are different with "busy" having two syllables and "brief" having one.

Verse 1, Line 1 has an extra syllable at the end "y" and Verse 1, Line 3 has an extra syllable at the beginning "if". Do I want to allow the extra syllables or work on a rewrite? When we syllabalize the other verses, we'll see if they have an extra syllable in the same places.

STEP 2

In the previous step, we wanted to know if the variations in Verse 1, Lines 1 and 3 matched in the other verses. Let's syllabalize Verse 2, Lines 1 and 3.

VERSE 2, LINE 1: Your Jaguar's fast, but you're running late

Row 1, Box 8 = "your"
Row 2, Box 1 = "Jag"
Row 2, Box 2 = "x"
Row 2, Box 3 = "uar's"

Row 2, Box 4 = "x"
Row 2, Box 5 = "fast"
Row 2, Boxes 6 and 7 = "x"
Row 2, Box 8 = "but"
Row 3, Box 1 = "you're"
Row 3, Box 2 = "run"
Row 3, Box 3 = "ning"
Row 3, Box 4 = "late"

Verse 2, Line 1 (double-time):

							your
Jag	x	uar's	x	fast	x	x	but
you're	run	ning	late				

VERSE 2, LINE 3: And you'll fly first-class, trying to achieve

Row 1, Box 6 = "and"
Row 1, Box 7 = "x"
Row 1, Box 8 = "you'll"
Row 2, Box 1 = "fly"
Row 2, Box 2 = "x"
Row 2, Box 3 = "first"
Row 2, Box 4 = "x"
Row 2, Box 5 = "class"
Row 2, Boxes 6, 7 and 8 = "x"
Row 3, Box 1 = "trying"
Row 3, Box 2 = "to"
Row 3, Box 3 = "a"
Row 3, Box 4 = "chieve"

Verse 2, Line 3 (double-time):

					and	x	you'll
fly	x	first	x	class	x	x	x
trying	to	a	chieve				

IDENTIFY PATTERNS

Verse 2, Line 1 (double-time):

							your
Jag	x	uar's	x	fast	x	x	but
you're	run	ning	late				

Verse 2, Line 3 (double-time):

					and	x	you'll
fly	x	first	x	class	x	x	x
trying	to	a	chieve				

Rows 1, Boxes 6 are different, with Verse 2, Line 3 having an additional pick-up syllable "and".

Rows 2 have identical phrasing.

Rows 2, Boxes 5 rhyme "fast" and "class".

Rows 3 have the same phrasing.

STEP 3

Before we compare Lines 1 and 3 of the first two verses, let's continue on to the odd lines in Verse 3.

VERSE 3, LINE 1: It's all a matter of priority, keep up what you're doing

Row 1, Box 2 = "it's"
Row 1, Box 3 = "all"
Row 1, Box 4 = "a"
Row 1, Box 5 = "mat"
Row 1, Box 6 = "ter"
Row 1, Box 7 = "of"
Row 1, Box 8 = "pri"

Row 2, Box 1 = "or"
Row 2, Box 2 = "x"
Row 2, Box 3 = "i"
Row 2, Box 4 = "x"
Row 2, Box 5 = "ty"

Verse 3, Line 1 (double-time):

	it's	all	a	mat	ter	of	pri
or	x	i	x	ty			

Row 2, Box 6 and 7 = "x"
Row 2, Box 8 = "keep"
Row 3, Box 1 = "up"
Row 3, Box 2 = "what"
Row 3, Box 3 = "you're"
Row 3, Box 4 = "do"
Row 3, Box 5 = "x"
Row 3, Box 6 = "ing"

Verse 3, Line 1 (double-time):

	it's	all	a	mat	ter	of	pri
or	x	i	x	ty	x	x	keep
up	what	you're	do	x	ing		

VERSE 3, LINE 3: With your family, you are their rock

Row 1, Box 6 = "with"
Row 1, Box 7 = "x"
Row 1, Box 8 = "your"
Row 2, Box 1 = "fam"
Row 2, Box 2 = "x"
Row 2, Box 3 = "i"
Row 2, Box 4 = "x"
Row 2, Box 5 = "ly"

Verse 3, Line 3 (double-time):

					with	x	your

fam	x	i	x	ly			

Row 2, Box 6, 7 and 8 = "x"
Row 3, Box 1 = "you"
Row 3, Box 2 = "are"
Row 3, Box 3 = "their"
Row 3, Box 4 = "rock"

Verse 3, Line 3 (double-time):

					with	x	your
fam	x	i	x	ly	x	x	x
you	are	their	rock				

IDENTIFY PATTERNS

Verse 3, Line 1 (double-time):

	it's	all	a	mat	ter	of	pri
or	x	i	x	ty	x	x	keep
up	what	you're	do	x	ing		

Verse 3, Line 3 (double-time):

					with	x	your
fam	x	i	x	ly	x	x	x
you	are	their	rock				

Rows 1 are different with a lot of variation. But since this line follows directly after the Bridge, it may work depending on the line before. We'll circle back to this a bit later.

Rows 2, Boxes 5 rhyme "priority" and "family".

Rows 2 have identical phrasing except Boxes 8. Verse 3, Line 1 has an additional pick-up syllable "keep".

Rows 3, Boxes 6 are different with "doing" having two syllables and "rock" having one.

STEP 4

Back in Step 1, we discovered that the end of Verse 1, Line 1 has two syllables "busy" while Verse 1, Line 3 has one syllable "brief". We also found Verse 1, Line 3 has an extra syllable at the beginning "if". We wanted to know if the other verses had the same variations.

To find out if the same variations are in the other verses, we syllabized the other odd lines in Steps 2 and 3. Next we'll compare the odd lines of all the verses together (not including the tag Lines 5).

Verse 1, Line 1 (double-time):

							your
child	-	gets	x	tall	x	x	x
while	you	are	bus	x	y		

Verse 1, Line 3 (double-time):

					if	x	you're
miss	ing	it	x	all	x	x	x
child	hood	is	brief				

Verse 2, Line 1 (double-time):

							your
Jag	x	uar's	x	fast	x	x	but
you're	run	ning	late				

Verse 2, Line 3 (double-time):

					and	x	you'll
fly	x	first	x	class	x	x	x
trying	to	a	chieve				

Verse 3, Line 1 (double-time):

	it's	all	a	mat	ter	of	pri
or	x	i	x	ty	x	x	keep

up	what	you're	do	x	ing		

Verse 3, Line 3 (double-time):

					with	x	your
fam	x	i	x	ly	x	x	x
you	are	their	rock				

In Lines 1, all Rows 1 are the same, except Verse 3 has a major variation, with six extra syllables.

In Lines 3, all Rows 1 are the same.

Rows 2, Boxes 2 have a variation in Verse 1, with extra syllables "-" and "ing".

Rows 2, Boxes 8 have a variation, with additional syllables in Verse 2, Line 1 "but" and Verse 3, Line 1 "keep". These variations are in the middle of a line, but functionally they act as pick-up syllables in the sentence.

Rows 3, Boxes 6 have a variation, with an additional syllable in Verse 1, Line 1 "busy" and Verse 3, Line 1 "doing".

Pick-up and tag syllables have minor impact in a sentence. I feel comfortable leaving the variations because I think they are negligible and add a little texture. There's prosody in leaving imperfections in a song called Perfect Enough.

STEP 5

The odd verse lines are syllabalized. Next grid the even lines. Work on Verse 1, Lines 2 and 4. Then continue with the even lines of the other verses. Begin by putting the even lines of Verse 1 in the grid.
VERSE 1, LINE 2: Think of it, isn't it really a shame

Row 2, Box 1 = "think"
Row 2, Box 2 = "of"
Row 2, Box 3 = "it"
Row 2, Box 4 = "is"
Row 2, Box 5 = "x"
Row 2, Box 6 = "n't"
Row 2, Box 7 = "x"
Row 2, Box 8 = "it"

Verse 1, Line 2 (double-time):

think	of	it	is	x	n't	x	it

Row 3, Box 1 = "real"
Row 3, Box 2 = "ly"
Row 3, Box 3 = "a"
Row 3, Box 4 = "shame"

Verse 1, Line 2 (double-time):

think	of	it	is	x	n't	x	it
real	ly	a	shame				

VERSE 1, LINE 4: Picture books and loose teeth and that Little League game

Row 1, Box 6 = "pic"
Row 1, Box 7 = "x"
Row 1, Box 8 = "ture"
Row 2, Box 1 = "books"
Row 2, Box 2 = "and"
Row 2, Box 3 = "loose"
Row 2, Box 4 = "teeth"

Verse 1, Line 4 (double-time):

					pic	x	ture
books	and	loose	teeth				

Row 2, Box 5 = "x"
Row 2, Box 6 = "and"
Row 2, Box 7 = "x"
Row 2, Box 8 = "that"
Row 3, Box 1 = "Lit"
Row 3, Box 2 = "tle"
Row 3, Box 3 = "League"
Row 3, Box 4 = "game"

Verse 1, Line 4 (double-time):

					pic	x	ture
books	and	loose	teeth	x	and	x	that
Lit	tle	League	game				

IDENTIFY PATTERNS

Verse 1, Line 2 (double-time):

					n't	x	it
think	of	it	is	x	n't	x	it
real	ly	a	shame				

Verse 1, Line 4 (double-time):

					pic	x	ture
books	and	loose	teeth	x	and	x	that
Lit	tle	League	game				

Rows 1 are different, with Verse 2, Line 4 having an additional two syllables in Boxes 6 and 8 "picture". We'll compare this to the other even lines to see if they have the same pattern.

Rows 2 and 3 have identical phrasing.

Rows 3, Boxes 4 rhyme "shame" and "game".
Verse 1, Line 4 has a triple alliteration "loose", "Little" and "League".

STEP 6

With Verse 1 complete, go on to the even lines of Verse 2.

VERSE 2, LINE 2: You won't catch the plane, but you'll get on the next

Row 1, Box 8 = "you"
Row 2, Box 1 = "won't"
Row 2, Box 2 = "catch"
Row 2, Box 3 = "the"
Row 2, Box 4 = "plane"

Verse 2, Line 2 (double-time):

							you
won't	catch	the	plane				

Row 2, Box 5 = "x"
Row 2, Box 6 = "but"
Row 2, Box 7 = "x"
Row 2, Box 8 = "you'll"
Row 3, Box 1 = "get"
Row 3, Box 2 = "on"
Row 3, Box 3 = "the"
Row 3, Box 4 = "next"

Verse 2, Line 2 (double-time):

							you
won't	catch	the	plane	x	but	x	you'll
get	on	the	next				

VERSE 2, LINE 4: The American Dream, while you're piling up debts

Row 1, Box 6 = "the"
Row 1, Box 7 = "x"
Row 1, Box 8 = "A"
Row 2, Box 1 = "mer"

112

Row 2, Box 2 = "i"
Row 2, Box 3 = "can"
Row 2, Box 4 = "dream"

Verse 2, Line 4 (double-time):

					the	x	A
mer	i	can	dream				

Row 2, Box 5 = "x"
Row 2, Box 6 = "while"
Row 2, Box 7 = "x"
Row 2, Box 8 = "you're"
Row 3, Box 1 = "pil"
Row 3, Box 2 = "ing"
Row 3, Box 3 = "up"
Row 3, Box 4 = "debts"

Verse 2, Line 4 (double-time):

					the	x	A
mer	i	can	dream	x	while	x	you're
pil	ing	up	debts				

IDENTIFY PATTERNS

Verse 2, Line 2 (double-time):

							you
won't	catch	the	plane	x	but	x	you'll
get	on	the	next				

Verse 2, Line 4 (double-time):

					the	x	A
mer	i	can	dream	x	while	x	you're
pil	ing	up	debts				

Rows 1, Boxes 6 are different, with Verse 2, Line 4 having an additional syllable "the".

Rows 2 and 3 have identical phrasing.

Rows 3, Boxes 4 has a near rhyme "next" and "debts".

STEP 7

Syllabalize the even lines of Verse 3.

VERSE 3, LINE 2: If it doesn't ruin the time that you spend

Row 1, Box 8 = "if"
Row 2, Box 1 = "it"
Row 2, Box 2 = "does"
Row 2, Box 3 = "n't"
Row 2, Box 4 = "ru"
Row 2, Box 5 = "x"
Row 2, Box 6 = "in"

Verse 3, Line 2 (double-time):

							if
it	does	n't	ru	x	in		

Row 2, Box 7 = "x"
Row 2, Box 8 = "the"
Row 3, Box 1 = "time"
Row 3, Box 2 = "that"
Row 3, Box 3 = "you"
Row 3, Box 4 = "spend"

Verse 3, Line 2 (double-time):

							if
it	does	n't	ru	x	in	x	the
time	that	you	spend				

114

VERSE 3, LINE 4: And they love when you walk through that door at the end

Row 1, Box 6 = "and"
Row 1, Box 7 = "x"
Row 1, Box 8 = "they"
Row 2, Box 1 = "love"
Row 2, Box 2 = "when"
Row 2, Box 3 = "you"
Row 2, Box 4 = "walk"

Verse 3, Line 4 (double-time):

					and	x	they
love	when	you	walk				

Row 2, Box 5 = "x"
Row 2, Box 6 = "through"
Row 2, Box 7 = "x"
Row 2, Box 8 = "that"
Row 3, Box 1 = "door"
Row 3, Box 2 = "at"
Row 3, Box 3 = "the"
Row 3, Box 4 = "end"

Verse 3, Line 4 (double-time):

					and	x	they
love	when	you	walk	x	through	x	that
door	at	the	end				

IDENTIFY PATTERNS

Verse 3, Line 2 (double-time):

							if
it	does	n't	ru	x	in	x	the
time	that	you	spend				

Verse 3, Line 4 (double-time):

					and	x	they
love	when	you	walk	x	through	x	that
door	at	the	end				

Rows 1, Boxes 6 are different, with Verse 3, Line 4 having an additional syllable "and".

Rows 2 and 3 have the same phrasing.

Rows 3, Boxes 4 rhyme "spend" and "end".

STEP 8

Look at the even lines from all the verses at once and compare patterns.

Verse 1, Line 2 (double-time):

think	of	it	is	x	n't	x	it
real	ly	a	shame				

Verse 1, Line 4 (double-time):

					pic	x	ture
books	and	loose	teeth	x	and	x	that
Lit	tle	League	game				

Verse 2, Line 2 (double-time):

							you
won't	catch	the	plane	x	but	x	you'll
get	on	the	next				

Verse 2, Line 4 (double-time):

					the	x	A

mer	i	can	dream	x	while	x	you're
pil	ing	up	debts				

Verse 3, Line 2 (double-time):

							if
it	does	n't	ru	x	in	x	the
time	that	you	spend				

Verse 3, Line 4 (double-time):

					and	x	they
love	when	you	walk	x	through	x	that
door	at	the	end				

In Lines 2, all Rows 1 are the same, except Verse 1 has no pick-up syllable.

In Lines 4, all Rows 1 are the same.

Everything else has identical phrasing. This increases memorability.

STEP 9

Write the tag line of the verses into the grid and look at the patterns.

VERSE 1, LINE 5: Man, relax
VERSE 2, LINE 5: Man, relax

Row 1, Box 6 = "man"
Row 1, Box 7 = "re"
Row 1, Box 8 = "lax"

Verses 1 & 2, Line 5 (double-time):

					man	re	lax

VERSE 3, LINE 5: Of the day

Row 1, Box 6 = "of"
Row 1, Box 7 = "the"
Row 1, Box 8 = "day"

Verse 3, Line 5 (double-time):

					of	the	day

IDENTIFY PATTERNS

Verses 1 and 2, Line 5 (double-time):

					man	re	lax

Verse 3, Line 5 (double-time):

					of	the	day

Verses 1 and 2, Lines 5 have identical words.

All Lines 5 have the same phrasing.

STEP 10

Look at each verse as a whole and compare the verses to each other.

Verse 1 (double-time):

								your
child	-	gets	x	tall	x	x	x
while	you	are	bus	x	y	x	x
think	of	it	is	x	n't	x	it
real	ly	a	shame	x	if	x	you're
miss	ing	it	x	all	x	x	x
child	hood	is	brief	x	pic	x	ture

books	and	loose	teeth	x	and	x	that
Lit	tle	League	game	x	man	re	lax

Verse 2 (double-time):

							your
Jag	x	uar's	x	fast	x	x	but
you're	run	ning	late	x	x	x	you
won't	catch	the	plane	x	but	x	you'll
get	on	the	next	x	and	x	you'll
fly	x	first	x	class	x	x	x
trying	to	a	chieve	x	the	x	A
mer	i	can	dream	x	while	x	you're
pil	ing	up	debts	x	man	re	lax

Verse 3 (double-time):

	it's	all	a	mat	ter	of	pri
or	x	i	x	ty	x	x	keep
up	what	you're	do	x	ing	x	if
it	does	n't	ru	x	in	x	the
time	that	you	spend	x	with	x	your
fa	x	mi	x	ly	x	x	x
you	are	their	rock	x	and	x	they
love	when	you	walk	x	through	x	that
door	at	the	end	x	of	the	day

Rows 1 are the same, except Verse 3, which has six extra syllables. The variation comes directly after the Bridge, which is a section meant to be different, and it may work in context. We'll circle back after syllabalizing the Bridge and see if I'll allow it.

Rows 2 are different in Verse 1 than the other verses with an extra syllable in Row 2, Box 2 "-" and no syllable in Box 8 "x".

Rows 3, Boxes 6 have a variation, with Verse 2 having no syllable "x".

Rows 3, Boxes 8 have a variation, with Verse 1 having no syllable "x".

Rows 4 and 5 are identical.

Rows 6 have a variation in Box 2, with Verse 1 having an extra syllable in "missing".

Rows 7, 8, 9 are identical.

Rows 3, Boxes 4, 5, 6 have internal near rhymes with Rows 4, Boxes 4, 5, 6, "busy" and "isn't", "late" and "plane", "doing" and "ruin".

There are lots of variations, but I think it's perfect enough.

STEP 11

This is a short chorus with few syllables. It doesn't have much melodic repetition. We'll syllabalize the whole chorus in one step.

CHORUS, LINE 1: Life is perfect enough

Row 1, Box 5 = "life"
Row 1, Boxes 6 and 7 = "x"
Row 1, Box 8 = "is"
Row 2, Box 1 = "per"
Row 2, Box 2 = "fect"
Row 2, Box 3 = "e"
Row 2, Box 4 = "nough"

120

Chorus (double-time):

				life	x	x	is
per	fect	e	nough				

CHORUS, LINE 2: Perfect enough, Lord

Row 2, Box 5, 6, 7 and 8 = "x"
Row 3, Boxes 1, 2, 3 and 4 = "x"
Row 3, Box 5 = "per"
Row 3, Box 6= "fect"
Row 3, Box 7 = "e"
Row 3, Box 8 = "nough"
Row 4, Box 1 and 2 = "x"
Row 4, Box 3 = "Lord"

Chorus (double-time):

				life	x	x	is
per	fect	e	nough	x	x	x	x
x	x	x	x	per	fect	e	nough
x	x	Lord					

CHORUS, LINE 3: It could be better, sometimes it's rough

Row 4, Box 4, 5, 6, 7 and 8 = "x"
Row 5, Box 1 = "x"
Row 5, Box 2 = "it"
Row 5, Box 3 = "could"
Row 5, Box 4 = "be"
Row 5, Box 5 = "bet"
Row 5, Box 6 = "ter"
Row 5, Box 7 = "x"
Row 5, Box 8 = "some"
Row 6, Box 1 = "x"
Row 6, Box 2 = "times"
Row 6, Box 3 = "it's"
Row 6, Box 4 = "rough"

Chorus (double-time):

				life	x	x	is
per	fect	e	nough	x	x	x	x
x	x	x	x	per	fect	e	nough
x	x	Lord	x	x	x	x	x
x	it	could	be	bet	ter	x	some
x	times	it's	rough				

CHORUS, LINE 4: But today is perfect enough

Row 6, Box 5 = "x"
Row 6, Box 6 = "but"
Row 6, Box 7 = "to"
Row 6, Box 8 = "day"
Row 7, Box 1, 2 and 3 = "x"
Row 7, Box 4 = "is"
Row 7, Box 5 = "per"
Row 7, Box 6 = "fect"
Row 7, Box 7 = "e"
Row 7, Box 8 = "nough"

Chorus (double-time):

				life	x	x	is
per	fect	e	nough	x	x	x	x
x	x	x	x	per	fect	e	nough
x	x	Lord	x	x	x	x	x
x	it	could	be	bet	ter	x	some
x	times	it's	rough	x	but	to	day
x	x	x	is	per	fect	e	nough

IDENTIFY PATTERNS

Chorus (double-time):

				life	x	x	is
per	fect	e	nough	x	x	x	x

x	x	x	x	per	fect	e	nough
x	x	Lord	x	x	x	x	x
x	it	could	be	bet	ter	x	some
x	times	it's	rough	x	but	to	day
x	x	x	is	per	fect	e	nough

Chorus, Lines 1 and 3 begin on Boxes 5, long after the downbeat. This is a big contrast to the verses beginning before the downbeat.

There are a lot of empty boxes, especially comparing to the busy verses. Making song sections distinct from each other is an established songwriting technique. Contrast between song sections stimulates interest.

The title hook "Perfect Enough" has four syllables in consecutive boxes. This phrasing repeats three times.

Row 2, Box 4 and Row 6, Box 4 rhyme "enough" and "rough". Rhyming a hook strengthens it since the repetition of sound increases memorability.

STEP 12

The final part we need to complete is the bridge. Stay in double-time to make the syncopated lyrics easier to analyze.
BRIDGE, LINE 1: You should be proud of what you've done

Row 1, Box 1 = "you"
Row 1, Box 2 = "should"
Row 1, Box 3 = "be"
Row 1, Box 4 = "proud"
Row 1, Box 5 = "x"
Row 1, Box 6 = "of"
Row 1, Box 7 = "what"
Row 1, Box 8 = "you've"

Row 2, Box 1 = "done"

Bridge (double-time):

you	shoul d	be	proud	x	of	what	you'v e
done							

BRIDGE, LINE 2: Look how far you've come

Row 2, Box 2, 3 and 4 = "x"
Row 2, Box 5 = "look"
Row 2, Box 6 = "how"
Row 2, Box 7 = "far"
Row 2, Box 8 = "you've"
Row 3, Box 1 = "come"

Bridge (double-time):

you	should	be	proud	x	of	what	you've
done	x	x	x	look	how	far	you've
come							

IDENTIFY PATTERNS

Bridge (double-time):

you	should	be	proud	x	of	what	you've
done	x	x	x	look	how	far	you've
come							

Both lines have groupings of four or five syllables in consecutive boxes.

Rows 1 and 2, Boxes 1 have a near-rhyme "done" and "come".

Bridge, Line 1 is much longer than Bridge, Line 2. It's okay to be lopsided in a Bridge, which is a section meant to be a departure from the rest of the song.

STEP 13

Back in Step 1, we wanted to know how the bridge flows into the extra-long pick-up of Verse 3, Line 1 "it's all a matter of". Put the bridge together with the preceding verse to see how they fit together.

Bridge, Line 2 & Verse 3, Line 1 (double-time):

				look	how	far	you've
come	x	x	x	x	x	x	x
x	it's	all	a	mat	ter	of	pri
or	x	i	x	ty			

Because Bridge, Line 2 is so short, there's plenty of room before the next verse begins. Verse 3, Line 1 would fit on Row 2, but I gave it even more room and started it on Row 3. The bridge would feel short with only two unbalanced lines, but a traditional four bars make it more palatable.

Effectively, I treat the first half of Verse 3, Line 1 as if it was the Bridge, Line 3. It all locks in together. It was instinct that made me balance out the bridge by adding an extra-long pick-up after a truncated line. Instinct fit the lines together and I used syllabalizing to "check the math"

SUMMARY

In Chapter 6, you practiced how to:
- Syllabalize in double-time
- Compare and identify patterns

The previous song took twenty-two steps and this one only took thirteen. We'll continue to accelerate as you become accustomed to syllabalizing.

Let's look at the song as a whole.

Perfect Enough (double-time):

							your
child	-	gets	x	tall	x	x	x
while	you	are	bus	x	y	x	x
think	of	it	is	x	n't	x	it
real	ly	a	shame	x	if	x	you're
miss	ing	it	x	all	x	x	x
child	hood	is	brief	x	pic	x	ture
books	and	loose	teeth	x	and	x	that
Lit	tle	League	game	x	man	re	lax
x	x	x	x	life	x	x	_is_
per	fect	e	nough	x	x	x	x
x	x	x	x	per	fect	e	nough
x	x	Lord	x	x	x	x	x
x	it	could	be	bet	ter	x	some
x	times	it's	rough	x	but	to	day
x	x	x	is	per	fect	e	nough
x	x	x	x	x	x	x	your
Jag	x	uar's	x	fast	x	x	but
you're	run	ning	late	x	x	x	you
won't	catch	the	plane	x	but	x	you'll
get	on	the	next	x	and	x	you'll
fly	x	first	x	class	x	x	x
trying	to	a	chieve	x	the	x	A
mer	i	can	dream	x	while	x	you're
pil	ing	up	debts	x	man	re	lax
x	x	x	x	life	x	x	_is_
per	fect	e	nough	x	x	x	x
x	x	x	x	per	fect	e	nough
x	x	Lord	x	x	x	x	x
x	it	could	be	bet	ter	x	some
x	times	it's	rough	x	but	to	day
x	x	x	is	per	fect	e	nough
x	x	x	x	x	x	x	x
you	should	be	proud	x	of	what	you've
done	x	x	x	look	how	far	you've
come	x	x	x	x	x	x	x

x	It's	all	a	mat	ter	of	pri
or	x	i	x	ty	x	x	keep
up	what	you're	do	x	ing	x	if
it	does	n't	ru	x	in	x	the
time	that	you	spend	x	with	x	your
fam	x	i	x	ly	x	x	x
you	are	their	rock	x	and	x	they
love	when	you	walk	x	through	x	that
door	at	the	end	x	of	the	day
x	x	x	x	life	x	x	<u>is</u>
per	fect	e	nough	x	x	x	x
x	x	x	x	per	fect	e	nough
x	x	Lord	x	x	x	x	x
x	it	could	be	bet	ter	x	some
x	times	it's	rough	x	but	to	day
x	x	x	is	per	fect	e	nough

EXERCISE

1. Write down the lyrics of a song.

2. Tap your finger from left to right and sing in time. If there are lots of boxes with more than one syllable in them, grid in double-time.

3. When you sing each syllable, see which box your finger is touching, and write the syllable in the box.

4. When all the lyrics are in the grid, identify patterns. Which lines match? Do the verses match? Is the chorus similar or different from the verse pattern? Where are the rhymes?

CHAPTER 7
SOLVE A RHYME

In previous chapters, we used a grid to identify patterns. You observed how writing in a grid is helpful for fine-tuning lyrics and pinpointing word problems. We talked extensively about using the method for rewriting. But for a moment, let's veer off and explore how to use it at the beginning of the writing process. I'll show you how to write lyrics in a grid while creating a song from scratch.

Say you experience a spark of inspiration propelling you to write a song. You may only have a few words or a story idea, a hook or a melody fragment. You haven't written anything yet, there's no draft to lay in a grid, as you did in the previous chapters. How can syllabalizing be used while creating a song?

Before I show you how to create a song from scratch using a grid, let's back way up and state the fundamentals. What is a song made of? For the purposes of this discussion, a song is basically made of five elements:
1. Story
2. Hook
3. Words
4. Melody
5. Music

There are multiple ways to approach writing a song, depending on the order of the elements. Whether you pay attention or not, you most certainly have a tendency to prefer a particular order. You may start with a hook and then brainstorm words (2 > 3). Or you may start with words and then write melody (3 > 4). It's also common to begin with a music track, then write words and melody at the same time (5 > 3 + 4). When it comes to the process of writing a song, there are many possibilities of the order of elements.

Most professionals have mastered multiple elements. They can switch up the order and use more than one element simultaneously. These experts do it all without even thinking about it. But pretty much all songwriters, again without thinking about it, get into a habit of writing in one order. Mind you, there is no right order, it's all artistic choice. But it's helpful to recognize your own tendencies.

Know yourself. Are you comfortable with all the elements or do you excel in one? Do you easily come up with melodies but get stuck on words (strong 4, weak 3)? Do you write lyrics prolifically but can't compose music (strong 3, weak 5)? It's perfectly fine to be good at one or two elements. You can find cowriters who are strong where you are weak. You can be a specialist and focus on your strength.

On the other hand, you may want to put more effort into improving the elements that aren't strong, becoming a more well-rounded writer. Either way, it's your choice, art isn't about right and wrong. It's just a good idea to know what you bring to the table, rather than being unconscious.

Know yourself. When you start a song, is there an element you prefer to begin with? Do you usually start with a music track and then find a melody and then write words (5 > 4 > 3)? Do you prefer to begin with the hook and then write words and then come up with a melody (2 > 3 > 4)? Or do you write words and melody at the same time and then work on the story (3 + 4 > 1)?

Having a preference for order is neither good nor bad, it's just important to be aware of it. When you don't consciously think about the elements and their order, you can fall into a habit you're unable to alter. Being aware of your tendencies promotes greater flexibility and options.

I know myself; my strength is story and words (1 + 3). My tendency is to begin with a story concept, then find a hook, then write words and melody at the same time (1 > 2 > 3 + 4). I've had a lot of practice writing every element, in every order. I refer to it as the ability to "approach a song from any angle".

It's beneficial to be able to "approach a song from any angle", to write in any order of elements. The skill is especially useful when co-writing. When you can recognize a cowriter's preferences, and be flexible enough to change your own tendencies, you become an agreeable writing partner.

Imagine you're observing me and I'm going to write the song Perfect Enough. You already know the song from Chapter 6 (Learn The Song, page 99) but say I haven't written anything yet. How do I start? I start with my preference, the story concept (element 1). As you remember, the story is about giving advice to a friend, telling him his drive to succeed is making him miss out on his family.

With an idea for the story, I go looking for a hook (1 > 2). I have an imaginary conversation with my friend and out comes the sentence "man relax, life is perfect enough". I latch onto it, that's a hook.
With the story and hook sketched out, I'm going to write words, lots of them (1 > 2 > 3). I take out a notebook and write the first words that occur to me:

> Your child gets tall
> It's kind of a shame
> If you miss it all
> That Little League game

The line "your child gets tall" is powerful because it conveys the core idea that time with a child is fleeting.

I don't know about the line "it's kind of a shame", it sounds awkward. I want to rhyme "game" and brainstorm some alternatives: "it's an awful shame", "what a terrible shame", "it's a dog-gone shame". I try other rhymes, like "aim", "blame", "came", "claim", "fame", "flame", "name", "same", and a bunch of near rhymes, including "pain", "drain", "stain", "rain", "explain".

Maybe you think I'm over-exaggerating the amount of writing going into one small line. If anything, I'm under-exaggerating. I write dozens of pages for each three-minute song. Maybe you think going to such a level of detail is unnecessary and you can name great songs entirely completed in a brief flash of inspiration. You'd be right to think it and I'm a prime example. I wrote my most successful song King Of Kings in under an hour when I was a child. Success in the music business is quirky at best.

But if I were to guess, I'd say you are like me. I think you care about words as deeply as I do, otherwise you wouldn't have made it this far into reading a dry text book such as this one. There's no such thing as a small line, that's foreign to people like us. Every line, every word, every syllable counts.

I love re-writing and confess to being an over-writer. The funny thing is, I often find myself returning to my first instinct. Even so, over-writing is not a waste of time, if only to prove my instincts were right. In the case of Verse 1, Line 2, I still think "shame" is the best rhyme. It evokes the right emotion and provides a motivation for my friend to change his ways.

I'll put the syllable "shame" in the grid, even though I haven't decided on how to construct the sentence. You've heard of solving a riddle? Here we're solving a rhyme.

STEP I

Build a grid with the words we're trying to match. Leave the line we're working on empty.
VERSE 1, LINE 1: Your child gets tall
VERSE 1, LINE 2: ~~It's kind of a~~ shame
Row 1, Box 8 = "your"
134

Row 2, Box 1 = "child"
Row 2, Box 2 = "-"
Row 2, Box 3 = "gets"
Row 2, Box 4 = "x"
Row 2, Box 5 = "tall"
Row 3, Box 4 = "shame"

Verse 1:

							your
child	-	gets	x	tall			
			shame				

VERSE 1, LINE 3: If you're missing it all
VERSE 1, LINE 4: That Little League game

Row 3, Box 5 = "x"
Row 3, Box 6 = "if"
Row 3, Box 7 = "x"
Row 3, Box 8 = "you're"
Row 4, Box 1 = "miss"
Row 4, Box 2 = "ing"
Row 4, Box 3 = "it"
Row 4, Box 4 = "x"
Row 4, Box 5 = "all"
Row 4, Box 8 = "that"
Row 5, Box 1 = "Lit"
Row 5, Box 2 = "tle"
Row 5, Box 3 = "league"
Row 5, Box 4 = "game"

Verse 1:

							your
child	-	gets	x	tall			
			shame	x	if	x	11
miss	ing	it	x	all			that
Lit	tle	League	game				

Actually, this looks short for a verse. Can I write a couple of extra lines at the end? I could but I feel "Little League game" is a strong image, not normally heard in a song. It evokes emotion and emphasizes the fleeting time of childhood. I really want this image to go right before the chorus because putting a strong image at the end of a verse makes it feel like a punch line. It opens the listener's ear right before going into the chorus, like salt opening taste buds.

Since I don't want to add lines at the end of the verse, can I put a few extra lines at the beginning? I could but I feel the first line "your child gets tall" is a great way to start the song. I love when a first line is a clue pointing to the overall meaning, without directly giving it away. I want this image at the top of the verse.

Leaving the first line "your child gets tall" and the last line "Little League game" in place, where can I add a few extra rows? Obviously, the only place left is in the middle. Let's add two rows, we can always add more later.

Insert two rows after Row 2.

Verse 1:

							your
child	-	gets	x	tall			
			shame		if	x	you're
miss	ing	it	x	all			that
Lit	tle	League	game				

STEP 2

With the added lines in Rows 3 and 4, I need to write for the empty boxes. The first line "your child gets tall" is an unfinished thought. Complete the sentence by adding "while you are busy".

VERSE 1, LINE 1: Your child gets tall while you are busy

Row 2, Boxes 6 to 8 = "x"
Row 3, Box 1 = "while"
Row 3, Box 2 = "you"
Row 3, Box 3 = "are"
Row 3, Box 4 = "bus"
Row 3, Box 5 = "x"
Row 3, Box 6 = "y"

Verse 1:

								your
child	-	gets	x	tall	x	x	x	
while	you	are	bus	x	y			
			shame	x	if	x		you're
miss	ing	it	x	all				that
Lit	tle	League	game					

IDENTIFY PATTERNS

Verse 1:

								your
child	-	gets	x	tall	x	x	x	
while	you	are	bus	x	y			
			shame	x	if	x		you're
miss	ing	it	x	all				that
Lit	tle	League	game					

I want to find a rhyme for "busy". I'm a sucker for internal rhymes and the melody lends itself to repeating in that place. After some consideration, I settle on the near rhyme "isn't".

STEP 3

To strengthen the internal near rhyme "busy" and "isn't", we're repeating the phrasing of Row 3 in Row 4. We're not matching odd and even lines here because the internal rhyme is on consecutive lines.

Microscopically examine Row 3. Solve for the internal rhyme "busy" and "isn't". The rhyme is the starting point.

Put the rhyme "isn't" in Row 4, directly underneath "busy" in Row 3.

Row 4, Box 4 = "is"
Row 4, Box 5 = "x"
Row 4, Box 6 = "n't"

Verse 1:

							your
child	-	gets	x	tall	x	x	x
while	you	are	bus	x	y		
			is	x	n't		

Let's make it a bit more conversational by saying "isn't it".

Row 4, Box 6 = "x"
Row 4, Box 7 = "it"

Verse 1:

							your
child	-	gets	x	tall	x	x	x

while	you	are	bus	x	y		
			is	x	n't	x	it

Continue solving the rhyme by working backwards from "isn't". Repeat the pattern in Row 3, Boxes 1, 2 and 3 "while you are" into Row 4, Boxes 1, 2 and 3. Use the placeholder "dah".

Row 4, Boxes 1 to 3 = "dah"

Verse 1:

							your
child	-	gets	x	tall	x	x	x
while	you	are	bus	x	y		
dah	dah	dah	is	x	n't	x	it

What three syllables can come before "isn't it"? After experimenting with possibilities, I'm going to use "think of it" to make it sound personal and conversational.

Row 2, Box 3 = "it"
Row 2, Box 3 = "of"
Row 2, Box 3 = "think"

Verse 1:

							your
child	-	gets	x	tall	x	x	x
while	you	are	bus	x	y		
think	of	it	is	x	n't	x	it

STEP 4

Take a look at Verse 1 so far.

Verse 1:

							your
child	-	gets	x	tall	x	x	x
while	you	are	bus	x	y	x	x
think	of	it	is	x	n't	x	it
			shame	x	if	x	you're
miss	ing	it	x	all			that
Lit	tle	League	game				

There's a blank space before "shame". I'm going with "really a shame" because it continues the conversational tone.

Work backwards from the rhyme "shame".

Row 5, Box 3 = "a"
Row 5, Box 2 = "ly"
Row 5, Box 1 = "real"

Verse 1:

							your
child	-	gets	x	tall	X	x	x
while	you	are	bus	x	y	x	x
think	of	it	is	x	n't	x	it
real	ly	a	sham e	x	if	x	you'r e
miss	ing	it	x	all			that
Lit	tle	League	game				

STEP 5

I'm happy with the first half of Verse 1. Compare it to the second half of the verse. Break it into two grids to see the patterns more clearly.

Verse 1, Lines 1 & 2:

							your
child	-	gets	x	tall	x	x	x
while	you	are	bus	x	y	x	x
think	of	it	is	x	n't	x	it
real	ly	a	shame				

Verse 1, Lines 3 & 4:

					if	x	you're
miss	ing	it	x	all			that
Lit	tle	League	game				

Rows 1 have pick-ups with a phrasing variation "your" and "if you're". I decide to ignore this variation because pick-up syllables have minor significance.

Rows 2, Boxes 5 rhyme "tall" and "all".

The first half has five rows and the second half has three rows. We previously lengthened the first half, making the second half off-kilter.

We want to leave the rhymes "all" in Row 2 and "game" in Row 5. Insert two rows after "missing it all" and before "Little League game". This will make the second half of the grid match the length of the first half.

Verse 1, Lines 3 & 4:

					if	x	you're
miss	ing	it	x	all			
							that
Lit	tle	League	game				

STEP 6

Match the internal near rhyme in Verse 1, Lines 1 and 2 "busy" and "isn't", repeating the pattern in Verse 1, Lines 3 and 4. Then solve for the new rhyme by putting another internal rhyme in the corresponding boxes.

Make a template by copying the first six boxes of Rows 3 and 4 from Lines 1 and 2, and pasting to Lines 3 and 4.

Verse 1, Lines 3 & 4:

					if	x	you're
miss	ing	it	x	all	x	x	x
while	you	are	bus	x	y		
think	of	it	is	x	n't		that
Lit	tle	League	game				

Use a two-syllable nonsense rhyme "polly" and "molly" as a placeholder. Write the placeholders in the same boxes as the first internal rhyme "busy" and "isn't".

Row 3, Box 4 = "pol"
Row 3, Box 5 = "x"
Row 3, Box 6 = "ly"
Row 4, Box 4 = "mol"
Row 4, Box 5 = "x"
Row 4, Box 6 = "ly"

Verse 1, Lines 3 & 4:

					if	x	you're
miss	ing	it	x	all	x	x	x
while	you	are	pol	x	ly		
think	of	it	mol	x	ly		that
Lit	tle	League	game				

Replace the rest of the pasted sentences in Rows 3 and 4 "while you are" and "think of it" with nonsense syllable "dah".

142

Rows 3 and 4, Boxes 1, 2 and 3 = "dah"

					if	x	you're
miss	ing	it	x	all	x	x	x
dah	dah	dah	pol	x	ly		
dah	dah	dah	mol	x	ly		that
Lit	tle	League	game				

Write new words to replace the nonsense. Unfiltered scribbling is a valuable practice to glean bits of brilliance from the subconscious mind. I keep random words and sentences in a "spare parts" file. I'm going to rummage through my junkyard of unused ideas to see if I can find a gem.

I find the phrase "childhood is brief". After spinning around a bunch of rhymes, I land on "loose teeth" and I'm excited to find an original and powerful image to support the fleeting time of childhood. The first internal rhyme "busy" and "isn't" have two syllables. The second internal rhyme "brief" and "teeth" have one syllable. But I don't care, a great line is a good reason to allow a variation.

Take out the placeholder rhyme "polly" and "molly" and replace it with "brief" and "teeth".

Row 3, Box 4 = "brief"
Row 4, Box 4 = "teeth"

Verse 1, Lines 3 & 4:

					if	x	you're
miss	ing	it	x	all	x	x	x
dah	dah	dah	brief				
dah	dah	dah	teeth				that
Lit	tle	League	game				

Work backwards from the rhyme "brief". There are three nonsense syllables "dah" in Row 3, Boxes 1, 2 and 3. This turns out to be the perfect amount of space to fit "childhood is".

Row 3, Box 3 = "is"
Row 3, Box 2 = "hood"
Row 3, Box 1 = "child"

Verse 1, Lines 3 and 4:

					if	x	you're
miss	ing	it	x	all	x	x	x
child	hood	is	brief				
dah	dah	dah	teeth				that
Lit	tle	League	game				

Work backwards from the rhyme "teeth" in Row 4, Box 4.

Row 4, Box 3 – "loose"

Verse 1, Lines 3 and 4:

					if	x	you're
miss	ing	it	x	all	x	x	x
child	hood	is	brief				
dah	dah	loose	teeth				that
Lit	tle	League	game				

There's space between "brief" and "loose teeth". What should we put there? Consider what the storyline needs. The philosophical statement "childhood is brief" is followed by two real and visual examples "loose teeth" and "Little League game". These are things that only happen for a very short period while growing up. The choice of words supports the core concept.

With two concrete examples of the brevity of childhood, all I need is one more example to complete the sentence. I come up with "picture books", another relic of childhood.

Work backwards from "loose teeth" in Row 4, Boxes 3 and 4 and fill in the preceding boxes.

Row 4, Box 2 = "and"
Row 4, Box 1 = "books"
Row 5, Box 8 = "ture"
Row 5, Box 7 = "x"
Row 5, Box 6 = "pic"
Row 5, Box 5 = "x"

Verse 1, Lines 3 & 4 (second half):

					if	x	you're
miss	ing	it	x	all	x	x	x
child	hood	is	brief	x	pic	x	ture
books	and	loose	teeth				that
Lit	tle	League	game				

IDENTIFY PATTERNS

To strengthen the new internal rhyme "brief" and "teeth", check for matching phrasing patterns in Rows 3 and 4.

Verse 1, Lines 3 & 4:

					if	x	you're
miss	ing	it	x	all	x	x	x
child	hood	is	brief	x	pic	x	ture
books	and	loose	teeth				that
Lit	tle	League	game				

The only variation in Rows 3 and 4 is in Boxes 6, with Row 3 having an extra syllable "pic". To make the rows match and keep the casual conversational tone, I'll add a filler word "and".
Row 4, Box 5 = "x"
Row 4, Box 6 = "and"
Row 4, Box 7 = "x"

Verse 1, Lines 3 & 4:

					if	x	you're
miss	ing	it	x	all	x	x	x
child	hood	is	brief	x	pic	x	ture
books	and	loose	teeth	x	and	x	that
Lit	tle	League	game				

STEP 7

Compare Verse 1, Lines 1 and 2 with Verse 1, Lines 3 and 4. See if the patterns match in the two halves or if there's variation.

Verse 1, Lines 1 & 2:

							your
child	-	gets	x	tall	x	x	x
while	you	are	bus	x	y	x	x
think	of	it	is	x	n't	x	it
real	ly	a	shame				

Verse 1, Lines 3 and 4:

					if	x	you're
miss	ing	it	x	all	x	x	x
child	hood	is	brief	x	pic	x	ture
books	and	loose	teeth	x	and	x	that
Lit	tle	League	game				

Rows 1, Boxes 6 have a variation, with Line 3 having an extra syllable "if".

Rows 2, Boxes 5 rhyme "tall" and "all"

Rows 3 and 4, boxes 4 have near-rhymes "busy" and "isn't", "brief" and "teeth".

146

Rows 3, Boxes 8 have a variation, with Verse 1, Lines 3 and 4 having an extra syllable "ture".

SUMMARY

In Chapter 7, you learned how to:
- Solve a rhyme by working backwards
- Use a grid to start a song from scratch
- Identify five elements of song composition
- Recognize writer tendencies

The explanation of syllabalizing is tedious and dry simply because it's very methodical. But after you get the hang of it, it's exciting to write in this new way of using visual patterns. Best of all, it's gratifying to hear the lyrics align and slide into the pocket.

EXERCISE

1. Write down the lyrics of a rhyming verse.

2. Tap your finger from left to right and sing the verse in time. If there are lots of boxes with more than one syllable in them, grid in double-time.

3. Write the syllables of the first rhyming line in the grid.

4. Find the corresponding row of the second rhyme and write that word in the same box number as the first rhyme.

5. Work backwards from the second rhyme, filling the boxes from right to left. Then tap from left to right and sing. Are the syllables in the correct boxes?

6. Identify patterns. Which lines match? Are the verses alike? Is the chorus identical or a variation from the verse pattern? Do the rhymes match?

CHAPTER 8
SOLVE ANOTHER RHYME

Say you're still in the writing room and I'm still working on Perfect Enough. The third verse is challenging. I rarely write a third verse in a song, but the storyline needs a conclusion after the bridge.

I go to my tendency, beginning with the story (element 1). I sketch out a storyboard, like a movie, summarizing each section in a single sentence. This helps me see the overview and figure out how to keep the lyrics focused on the core concept.

Here's the storyboard, up until the third verse:
- Verse 1: You're stressed all the time and missing out on your children growing up.
- Chorus: You should appreciate everything you have and take time to enjoy your family.
- Verse 2: The more money you spend, the more time you are required to work.
- Chorus: Don't chase material things and neglect what you already have.
- Bridge: You've done really well and should be proud of yourself.

I have to explain what I thinking when I wrote the bridge, it doesn't seem to fit in the rest of the storyboard. Up until the bridge, the song is about slowing down to appreciate life. But the bridge is saying the opposite, you're doing great, don't change. I need another verse to explain the bridge.

The backstory of the bridge originates with the friend who inspired the song. He is successful, with many achievements, and has to work hard. In my imaginary conversation with him, when he hears the suggestion to work fewer hours, he might feel defensive. I don't want to dismiss his accomplishments and I wrote the bridge to address the issue of balance.

The bridge goes off on a tangent and it needs to tie back into the core message. That's why I'm adding another verse. Here's the updated storyboard:

- <u>Verse 1</u>: You're stressed all the time and missing out on your children growing up.
- <u>Chorus</u>: You should appreciate everything you have and take time to enjoy your family.
- <u>Verse 2</u>: The more money you spend, the more time you are required to work.
- <u>Chorus</u>: Don't chase material things and neglect what you already have.
- <u>Bridge</u>: You've done really well and should be proud of yourself.
- <u>Verse 3</u>: It's a matter of balance and priorities, knowing how much your children need you.
- <u>Chorus</u>: Appreciate all you have and enjoy it.

With a clear idea for Verse 3, I brainstorm a draft about prioritizing family.

> Keep up what you're doing
> Just don't let it ruin
> The time that you've got
> With your family
> To them you're a rock
> They love when you walk
> In the house after work

There are some good ideas in the first draft, although it's rough. Writing the words in a grid will turn it into a strong verse.

<u>LINE NUMBERS</u>

VERSE 3, LINE 1: It's all a matter of priority, keep up what you're doing

VERSE 3, LINE 2: Just don't let it ruin the time that you've got
VERSE 3, LINE 3: With your family, to them you're a rock
VERSE 3, LINE 4: They love when you walk in the house after work

STEP 1

Verse 3 has the same melody as the other verses and I'll give it matching phrasing. Compare and precisely match the patterns of the first verse in the third verse. Begin with Verse 1 and this will create a template to build on.

Verse 1:

							your
child	-	gets	x	tall	x	x	x
while	you	are	bus	x	y	x	x
think	of	it	is	x	n't	x	it
real	ly	a	shame	x	if	x	you're
miss	ing	it	x	all	x	x	x
child	hood	is	brief	x	pic	x	ture
books	and	loose	teeth	x	and	x	that
Lit	tle	League	game	x	man	re	lax

Create a template for Verse 3 by replacing the external rhymes "tall" and "all" and "shame" and "game" with nonsense rhymes "pop" and "stop" and "shoe" and "glue".

Row 2, Box 5 = "pop"
Row 6, Box 5 = "stop"
Row 5, Box 4 = "rays"
Row 9, Box 4 = "days"

Verse 3:

							your

child	-	gets	x	pop	x	x	x
while	you	are	bus	x	y	x	x
think	of	it	is	x	n't	x	it
real	ly	a	shoe	x	if	x	you're
miss	ing	it	x	stop	x	x	x
child	hood	is	brief	x	pic	x	ture
books	and	loose	teeth	x	and	x	that
Lit	tle	League	glue	x	man	re	lax

Replace the internal rhymes "busy" and "isn't" and "brief" and "teeth" with placeholder rhymes "polly" and "molly" and "pay" and "say".

Row 3, Box 4 = "pol"
Row 3, Box 6 = "ly"
Row 4, Box 4 = "mol"
Row 4, Box 6 = "ly"
Row 7, Box 4 = "pay"
Row 8, Box 4 = "say"

Verse 3:

							your
child	-	gets	x	pop	x	x	x
while	you	are	pol	x	ly	x	x
think	of	it	mol	x	ly	x	it
real	ly	a	shoe	x	if	x	you're
miss	ing	it	x	stop	x	x	x
child	hood	is	pay	x	pic	x	ture
books	and	loose	say	x	and	x	that
Lit	tle	League	glue	x	man	re	lax

Now that the rhymes have placeholders, change the rest of the words to the nonsense syllable "dah". This creates the template we'll build on.

Verse 3:

							dah
dah	dah	dah	x	pop	x	x	x
dah	dah	dah	pol	x	ly	x	x
dah	dah	dah	mol	x	ly	x	it
dah	dah	dah	shoe	x	dah	x	dah
dah	dah	dah	x	stop	x	x	x
dah	dah	dah	pay	x	dah	x	dah
dah	dah	dah	say	x	dah	x	dah
dah	dah	dah	glue	x	dah	dah	dah

STEP 2

Find where to place the draft of Verse 3 into the right boxes by solving for the internal rhymes first. Start by replacing "polly" and "molly" with "doing" and "ruin".

VERSE 3, LINE 1: It's all a matter of priority, keep up what you're doing

VERSE 3, LINE 2: Just don't let it ruin the time that you've got

Row 3, Box 4 = "do"
Row 3, Box 6 = "ing"
Row 4, Box 4 = "ru"
Row 4, Box 6 = "in"

Verse 3:

							dah
dah	dah	dah	x	pop	x	x	x
dah	dah	dah	do	x	ing	x	x
dah	dah	dah	ru	x	in	x	dah
dah	dah	dah	shoe	x	if	x	dah
dah	dah	dah	x	stop	x	x	x

dah	dah	dah	pay	x	dah	x	dah
dah	dah	dah	say	x	dah	x	dah
dah	dah	dah	glue	x	dah	dah	dah

STEP 3

Solve for the internal rhyme "doing" and "ruin" by working backwards and filling in the lines.

VERSE 3, LINE 1: It's all a matter of priority, keep up what you're doing

Row 3, Box 3 = "you're"
Row 3, Box 2 = "what"
Row 3, Box 1 = "up"
Row 2, Box 8 = "keep"

Verse 3:

							dah
dah	dah	dah	x	pop	x	x	keep
up	what	you're	do	x	ing	x	x
dah	dah	dah	ru	x	in	x	dah
dah	dah	dah	shoe	x	if	x	dah
dah	dah	dah	x	stop	x	x	x
dah	dah	dah	pay	x	dah	x	dah
dah	dah	dah	say	x	dah	x	dah
dah	dah	dah	glue	x	dah	dah	dah

VERSE 3, LINE 2: Just don't let it ruin the time that you've got

Row 4, Box 3 = "it"
Row 4, Box 2 = "let"
Row 4, Box 1 = "don't"
Row 3, Box 8 = "just"

Verse 3:

							dah
dah	dah	dah	x	pop	x	x	keep
up	what	you're	do	x	ing	x	just
don't	let	it	ru	x	in	x	dah
dah	dah	dah	shoe	x	if	x	dah
dah	dah	dah	x	stop	x	x	x
dah	dah	dah	pay	x	dah	x	dah
dah	dah	dah	say	x	dah	x	dah
dah	dah	dah	glue	x	dah	dah	dah

STEP 4

The next internal rhyme is in Rows 7 and 8. Replace "pay" and "say" with "rock" and "walk".

VERSE 3, LINE 3: With your family, to them you're a rock
VERSE 3, LINE 4: They love when you walk in the house after work

Row 7, Box 4 = "rock"
Row 8, Box 4 = "walk"

Verse 3:

							dah
dah	dah	dah	x	pop	x	x	keep
up	what	you're	do	x	ing	x	just
don't	let	it	ru	x	in	x	dah
dah	dah	dah	shoe	x	if	x	dah
dah	dah	dah	x	stop	x	x	x
dah	dah	dah	rock	x	dah	x	dah
dah	dah	dah	walk	x	dah	x	dah
dah	dah	dah	glue	x	dah	dah	dah

STEP 5

Solve for the internal rhyme "rock" and "walk" by working backwards and filling in the lines.

VERSE 3, LINE 3: With your family, to them you're a rock

Row 7, Box 3 = "a"
Row 7, Box 2 = "you're"
Row 7, Box 1 = "them"
Row 6, Box 8 = "to"

Verse 3:

							dah
dah	dah	dah	x	pop	x	x	keep
up	what	you're	do	x	ing	x	just
don't	let	it	ru	x	in	x	dah
dah	dah	dah	shoe	x	if	x	dah
dah	dah	dah	x	stop	x	x	to
them	you're	a	rock	x	dah	x	dah
dah	dah	dah	walk	x	dah	x	dah
dah	dah	dah	glue	x	dah	dah	dah

VERSE 3, LINE 4: They love when you walk in the house after work

Row 8, Box 3 = "you"
Row 8, Box 2 = "when"
Row 8, Box 1 = "love"
Row 7, Box 8 = "they"

Verse 3:

							dah
dah	dah	dah	x	pop	x	x	keep
up	what	you're	do	x	ing	x	just
don't	let	it	ru	x	in	x	dah

dah	dah	dah	shoe	x	if	x	dah
dah	dah	dah	x	stop	x	x	to
them	you're	a	rock	x	dah	x	they
love	when	you	walk	x	dah	x	dah
dah	dah	dah	glue	x	dah	dah	dah

STEP 6

All the internal rhymes of Verse 3 have been matched. Next solve for the external rhymes. Begin with Rows 2 and 6 "pop" and "stop".

VERSE 3, LINE 3: With your family, to them you're a rock

We need a rhyme for "family". Fill in the word "family", starting with the rhyming syllable "ly" and working backwards.

Row 6, Box 5 = "ly"
Row 6, Box 3 = "i"
Row 6, Box 2 = "x"
Row 6, Box 1 = "fam"

Verse 3:

							dah
dah	dah	dah	x	pop	x	x	keep
up	what	you're	do	x	ing	x	just
don't	let	it	ru	x	in	x	dah
dah	dah	dah	shoe	x	if	x	dah
fam	x	i	x	ly	x	x	to
them	you're	a	rock	x	dah	x	they
love	when	you	walk	x	dah	x	dah
dah	dah	dah	glue	x	dah	dah	dah

STEP 7

In Row 6, we replaced "stop" with "family". We need a corresponding rhyme in Row 2. "Family" is an easy word to rhyme. There are many three and four syllable rhymes, like "happily", "basically", "naturally", "practically", "constantly", "honestly", "obviously", "primarily", "luckily".

I'm drawn to "priority" because it isn't usually heard in lyrics. I like that it has three hard vowels. Hard vowels are more fun to sing than soft ones. But most importantly, I like how the meaning is uniquely appropriate to the story concept of Verse 3, prioritizing family over materialism.

The rhyming syllables are in Row 6, Box 5 "ly" and Row 2, Box 5 "ty".

Row 2, Box 5 = "ty"

Verse 3:

							dah
dah	dah	dah	x	ty	x	x	keep
up	what	you're	do	x	ing	x	just
don't	let	it	ru	x	in	x	dah
dah	dah	dah	shoe	x	if	x	dah
fam	x	i	x	ly	x	x	to
them	you're	a	rock	x	dah	x	they
love	when	you	walk	x	dah	x	dah
dah	dah	dah	glue	x	dah	dah	dah

Work backwards from the rhyming syllable.

Row 2, Box 3 = "i"
Row 2, Box 2 = "x"
Row 2, Box 1 = "or"
Row 1, Box 8 = "pri"

Verse 3:

							pri
or	x	i	x	ty	x	x	keep
up	what	you're	do	x	ing	x	just
don't	let	it	ru	x	in	x	dah
dah	dah	dah	shoe	x	if	x	dah
fam	x	i	x	ly	x	x	to
them	you're	a	rock	x	dah	x	they
love	when	you	walk	x	dah	x	dah
dah	dah	dah	glue	x	dah	dah	dah

STEP 8

Work backwards from "family" to fill in the sentence.

VERSE 3, LINE 3: With your family, to them you're a rock

Row 5, Box 8 = "your"
Row 5, Box 6 = "with"

Verse 3:

							pri
or	x	i	x	ty	x	x	keep
up	what	you're	do	x	ing	x	just
don't	let	it	ru	x	in	x	dah
dah	dah	dah	shoe	x	with	x	your
fam	x	i	x	ly	x	x	to
them	you're	a	rock	x	dah	x	they
love	when	you	walk	x	dah	x	dah
dah	dah	dah	glue	x	dah	dah	dah

STEP 9

We'll make the word "priority" conversational by completing the sentence "it's all a matter of priority". This creates extra six syllables in a pick-up, a significant variation from the other verses. But it follows the bridge, where variations are welcome. Plus, we already know it fits from Chapter 6, Step 11.

Solve the rhyme by working backwards from "priority".

VERSE 3, LINE 1: It's all a matter of priority, keep up what you're doing

Row 1, Box 7 = "of"
Row 1, Box 6 = "ter"
Row 1, Box 5 = "mat"
Row 1, Box 4 = "a"
Row 1, Box 3 = "all"
Row 1, Box 2 = "it's"

Verse 3:

	it's	all	a	mat	ter	of	pri
or	x	i	x	ty	x	x	keep
up	what	you're	do	x	ing	x	just
don't	let	it	ru	x	in	x	dah
dah	dah	dah	shoe	x	with	x	your
fam	x	i	x	ly	x	x	to
them	you're	a	rock	x	dah	x	they
love	when	you	walk	x	dah	x	dah
dah	dah	dah	glue	x	dah	dah	dah

STEP 10

Complete Verse 1, Line 2, replacing the placeholder rhyme "shoe" and "glue".

VERSE 3, LINE 2: Just don't let it ruin the time that you've got

Beginning with the rhyming word "got".

Row 5, Box 4 = "got"

Verse 3:

	it's	all	a	mat	ter	of	pri
or	x	i	x	ty	x	x	keep
up	what	you're	do	x	ing	x	just
don't	let	it	ru	x	in	x	dah
dah	dah	dah	got	x	with	x	your
fam	x	i	x	ly	x	x	to
them	you're	a	rock	x	dah	x	they
love	when	you	walk	x	dah	x	dah
dah	dah	dah	glue	x	dah	dah	dah

Work backwards from the rhyme to fill in the sentence.

Row 5, Box 3 = "you've"
Row 5, Box 2 = "that"
Row 5, Box 1 = "time"
Row 4, Box 8 = "the"

Verse 3:

	it's	all	a	mat	ter	of	pri
or	x	i	x	ty	x	x	keep
up	what	you're	do	x	ing	x	just
don't	let	it	ru	x	in	x	the
time	that	you've	got	x	with	x	your
fam	x	i	x	ly	x	x	to
them	you're	a	rock	x	dah	x	they
love	when	you	walk	x	dah	x	dah
dah	dah	dah	glue	x	dah	dah	dah

STEP 11

We solved for the external rhyme "got" in Row 5. Now solve for "work" in Row 9. I'm going to rewrite this to get these lines to rhyme. But let's fill in the sentence as it is so we have the correct placement of syllables.

VERSE 3, LINE 4: They love when you walk in the house after work

Row 9, Box 4 = "work"

Verse 3:

	it's	all	a	mat	ter	of	pri
or	x	i	x	ty	x	x	keep
up	what	you're	do	x	ing	x	just
don't	let	it	ru	x	in	x	the
time	that	you've	got	x	with	x	your
fam	x	i	x	ly	x	x	to
them	you're	a	rock	x	dah	x	they
love	when	you	walk	x	dah	x	dah
dah	dah	dah	work	x	dah	dah	dah

Complete the sentence in Verse 3, Line 4, syllabalizing backwards.

Row 9, Box 3 = "ter"
Row 9, Box 2 = "af"
Row 9, Box 1 = "house"
Row 8, Box 8 = "the"
Row 8, Box 6 = "in"

Verse 3:

	it's	all	a	mat	ter	of	pri
or	x	i	x	ty	x	x	keep
up	what	you're	do	x	ing	x	just

don't	let	it	ru	x	in	x	the
time	that	you've	got	x	with	x	your
fam	x	i	x	ly	x	x	to
them	you're	a	rock	x	dah	x	they
love	when	you	walk	x	in	x	the
house	af	ter	work	x	dah	dah	dah

STEP 12

I need a rhyme for "got" or "work" and can't seem to find it. I must be tired and call it quits for the day. The following day I still can't figure out the rhyme and the next day I can't either. I set the song aside and make a decision to finish it later.

A few weeks pass and one morning I wake from a dream where the rhyme has been solved.

> It's all a matter of priority
> Keep up what you're doing
> If it doesn't ruin the time that you spend
> With your family, you are their rock
> And they love when you walk
> Through that door at the end of the day

While unconscious, I found a way around the rhyme problem by changing "got" to "spend". This is helpful because the original "you've got" was more difficult to sing with the consonants "v" and "g" next to each other. The new version "you spend" rolls off the tongue easier. Plus "spend" is a more interesting word than "got".

The dream rewrite "you are their rock" is better than the waking version "to them you're a rock". It's smoother and more conversational. Apparently, I'm a better songwriter when I'm asleep than when I'm awake.

Begin with the rhyme "got" and replace it with "spend".

VERSE 3, LINE 2: If it doesn't ruin the time that you spend

Row 5, Box 4 = "spend"

Verse 3:

	it's	all	a	mat	ter	of	pri
or	x	i	x	ty	x	x	keep
up	what	you're	do	x	ing	x	just
don't	let	it	ru	x	in	x	the
time	that	you've	spend	x	with	x	your
fam	x	i	x	ly	x	x	to
them	you're	a	rock	x	dah	x	they
love	when	you	walk	x	in	x	the
house	af	ter	work	x	dah	dah	dah

Work backwards from the rhyme to fill in the sentence.

Row 5, Box 3 = "you"

Verse 3:

	it's	all	a	mat	ter	of	pri
or	x	i	x	ty	x	x	keep
up	what	you're	do	x	ing	x	just
don't	let	it	ru	x	in	x	the
time	that	you	spend	x	with	x	your
fam	x	i	x	ly	x	x	to
them	you're	a	rock	x	dah	x	they
love	when	you	walk	x	in	x	the
house	af	ter	work	x	dah	dah	dah

Now change the beginning of the line from "just don't let it ruin" to "if it doesn't ruin". The rewrite is easier to sing.

Row 3, Box 8 = "if"
Row 4, Box 1 = "it"
Row 4, Box 2 = "does"
Row 4, Box 3 = "n't"

Verse 3:

	it's	all	a	mat	ter	of	pri
or	x	i	x	ty	x	x	keep
up	what	you're	do	x	ing	x	if
it	does	n't	ru	x	in	x	the
time	that	you	spend	x	with	x	your
fam	x	i	x	ly	x	x	to
them	you're	a	rock	x	dah	x	they
love	when	you	walk	x	in	x	the
house	af	ter	work	x	dah	dah	dah

Move on to Line 3. Work backwards from the rhyme "rock".

VERSE 3, LINE 3: With your family, you are their rock

Row 7, Box 3 = "their"
Row 7, Box 2 = "are"
Row 7, Box 1 = "you"
Row 6, Box 8 = "x"

Verse 3:

	it's	all	a	mat	ter	of	pri
or	x	i	x	ty	x	x	keep
up	what	you're	do	x	ing	x	if
it	does	n't	ru	x	in	x	the
time	that	you	spend	x	with	x	your
fam	x	i	x	ly	x	x	x
you	are	their	rock	x	dah	x	they
love	when	you	walk	x	in	x	the
house	af	ter	work	x	dah	dah	dah

VERSE 3, LINE 4: And they love when you walk

Row 7, Box 6 = "and"

Verse 3:

	it's	all	a	mat	ter	of	pri
or	x	i	x	ty	x	x	keep
up	what	you're	do	x	ing	x	if
it	does	n't	ru	x	in	x	the
time	that	you	spend	x	with	x	your
fam	x	i	x	ly	x	x	x
you	are	their	rock	x	and	x	they
love	when	you	walk	x	in	x	the
house	af	ter	work	x	dah	dah	dah

Complete the last line of the verse. Begin with the rhyme "end".

VERSE 3, LINE 5: Through that door at the end of the day

Row 9, Box 4 = "end"

Verse 3:

	it's	all	a	mat	ter	of	pri
or	x	i	x	ty	x	x	keep
up	what	you're	do	x	ing	x	if
it	does	n't	ru	x	in	x	the
time	that	you	spend	x	with	x	your
fam	x	i	x	ly	x	x	x
you	are	their	rock	x	and	x	they
love	when	you	walk	x	in	x	the
house	af	ter	end	x	dah	dah	dah

Work backwards from the rhyme to fill in the beginning of the sentence.

168

Row 9, Box 3 = "the"
Row 9, Box 2 = "at"
Row 9, Box 1 = "door"
Row 8, Box 8 = "that"
Row 8, Box 6 = "through"

Verse 3:

	it's	all	a	mat	ter	of	pri
or	x	i	x	ty	x	x	keep
up	what	you're	do	x	ing	x	if
it	does	n't	ru	x	in	x	the
time	that	you	spend	x	with	x	your
fam	x	i	x	ly	x	x	x
you	are	their	rock	x	and	x	they
love	when	you	walk	x	through	x	that
door	at	the	end	x	dah	dah	dah

Finish off the last part of the line, the new tag.

Row 9, Box 6 = "of"
Row 9, Box 7 = "the"
Row 9, Box 8 = "day"

Verse 3:

	it's	all	a	mat	ter	of	pri
or	x	i	x	ty	x	x	keep
up	what	you're	do	x	ing	x	if
it	does	n't	ru	x	in	x	the
time	that	you	spend	x	with	x	your
fam	x	i	x	ly	x	x	x
you	are	their	rock	x	and	x	they
love	when	you	walk	x	through	x	that
door	at	the	end	x	of	the	day

STEP 13

Double-check your work and make sure the patterns of the verses are matching.

Verse 1:

							your
child	-	gets	x	tall	x	x	x
while	you	are	bus	x	y	x	x
think	of	it	is	x	n't	x	it
real	ly	a	shame	x	if	x	you're
miss	ing	it	x	all	x	x	x
child	hood	is	brief	x	pic	x	ture
books	and	loose	teeth	x	and	x	that
Lit	tle	League	game	x	man	re	lax

Verse 2:

							your
Jag	x	uar's	x	fast	x	x	but
you're	run	ning	late	x	x	x	You
won't	catch	the	plane	x	but	x	you'll
get	on	the	next	x	and	x	you'll
fly	x	first	x	class	x	x	x
trying	to	a	chieve	x	the	x	A
mer	i	can	dream	x	while	x	you're
pil	ing	up	debts	x	man	re	lax

Verse 3:

	it's	all	a	mat	ter	of	pri
or	x	i	x	ty	x	x	keep
up	what	you're	do	x	ing	x	if
it	does	n't	ru	x	in	x	the
time	that	you	spend	x	with	x	your
fam	x	i	x	ly	x	x	x

you	are	their	rock	x	and	x	they
love	when	you	walk	x	through	x	that
door	at	the	end	x	of	the	day

The verses all match, except in Verse 2 where Row 3, Box 6 has no syllable, and in Verse 3 where Row 1 has more syllables.

In Verse 3, I substitute the three syllables "man relax" with "of the day". This dream solution solves another problem because I don't want to sing "man relax" three times, twice is plenty.

SUMMARY

In Chapter 8, you learned how to:
- Solve a rhyme by working backwards
- Use nonsense syllables and rhymes to build a template
- Build a storyboard by writing one sentence for each section of the song
- Remember your dreams, writing happens while you're asleep

To solve a rhyme, put the rhyming syllable in the box where it belongs. Work backwards from the rhyme to fit in the beginning of the sentence. Easy and effective.

EXERCISE

1. Write down the lyrics of a rhyming verse.

2. If there are lots of boxes with more than one syllable in them, grid in double-time. Tap from left to right and sing. Write each syllable in the box your finger is touching.

3. Create a template. Replace rhymes with nonsense rhymes, like "pop" and "stop" or "molly" and "polly". Replace the other words with nonsense syllables, like "dah".

4. Write a new verse with the same rhyme scheme. Replace the nonsense rhymes with the new rhymes.

5. Work backwards from the rhymes to fill in the lines.

CHAPTER 9
SOLVE A MELODY

In the previous chapters, you solved a rhyme. In this chapter, you'll solve a melody. Review the five basic elements of songwriting:

1. Story
2. Hook
3. Words
4. Melody
5. Music

You've been spending time with me in the writing room and witnessed my process. I usually start with a story concept, then find a hook, then build lyrics, (1>2>3). Even if I have a hook first, as in Rows Of Roses, I still prefer to build a storyline before writing words (2>1>3). This is my tendency, but there is no right way to start a song and you may prefer a different approach.

Books are linear, discussing one thing at a time, so I didn't tell you about the elements I'm working on simultaneously. We've been hammering out lyrics, focusing on story, hook and words (1>2>3). But actually, I'm simultaneously writing melody and working out chords. (1>2>3+4>5).

What is the value of breaking up a song into separate elements? Why should we go to such depths of analysis when it seems overly complicated? The thing is, it truly isn't complex, it's simple. Most of the time, songwriters achieve writing various elements at once, fluidly going back and forth between elements without thinking about it.

Instinct can be sufficient. More often than not, after strenuous rewrites, I find my first draft is my best draft. But syllabalizing goes beyond instinct to develop craft. The method is a granular technique, with the precision of a surgical incision. Breaking up the process into separate elements adds a layer of control.

STEP 1

We're still working on Perfect Enough, but now we'll focus on melody (Learn The Song, page 99). The hook "perfect enough" repeats three times. It has a melody that goes up in Chorus, Line 1 and then goes down in Chorus, Line 2. What am I going to do the third time, in Chorus, Line 4? It's an important decision because a repeated hook is the catchiest part of a song. Which hook melody do I want to repeat, the one going up or the one going down?

I try it both ways. When I go up, it sounds like a question "today is perfect enough?" Not the right meaning. When I go down, it sounds like I'm stating a fact "today is perfect enough!" That melody works better with the meaning.

The down hook melody has two notes. "Per" is on E and "fect enough" are on three C's. If we write the notes out, the following grid is how the down hook melody "E C C C" fits in a grid.

Row 3, Box 5 is "E".
Row 3, Box 6 is "C".
Row 3, Box 7 = "C"
Row 3, Box 8 = "C"
Row 7, Box 5 = "E"
Row 7, Box 6 = "C"
Row 7, Box 7 = "C"
Row 7, Box 8 = "C"

Chorus:

x	x	x	x	life	x	x	<u>is</u>
per	fect	e	nough	x	x	x	x

176

x	x	x	x	E	C	C	C
x	x	Lord	x	x	x	x	x
x	it	could	be	bet	ter	x	some
x	times	it's	rough	x	but	to	day
x	x	x	is	E	C	C	C

STEP 2

A common songwriting technique is to have the chorus melody soar above the rest of the notes, known as a vertical hook. But on this song, it doesn't rise, quite the opposite. It buttons up the end of the chorus with a feeling of closure, which was my artistic choice. To counteract the less memorable lower notes, I'll increase repetition to strengthen the melody.

In the music track, I write the hook melody into the instrumental at the beginning and interludes of the song. The whole instrumental is sprinkled with those notes "E C C C". In the verses, I find places to repeat the hook melody. It will be a little different because I don't want it to be exactly like the chorus, just a subtle echo to strengthen the memorability of the hook melody. But don't repeat the hook melody too often or the listener's ear will get fatigued.

Here's where the hook melody "E C C C" lands in the grid, using Verse 1 as an example. The melody is in the words "child gets tall" and "missing it all". Go back and listen for it in the track to hear it clearly. The repetition of melody was an intentional choice, not an improvisation.

Verse 1:

							your
E	C	C	x	C	x	x	x
while	you	are	bus	x	y	x	x
think	of	it	is	x	n't	x	it

real	ly	a	shame	x	if	x	you're
E	C	C	x	C	x	x	x
child	hood	is	brief	x	pic	x	ture
books	and	loose	teeth	x	and	x	that
Lit	tle	League	game	x	man	re	lax

SUMMARY

In Chapter 9, you learned how to:
- Solve a melody
- Repeat a hook melody
- Compensate for the lack of a vertical hook

Repeating a hook melody is a way of repeating a nugget of genius. Use this tip sparingly or it'll have the effect of making the hook feel repetitious and annoying.

Writing lyrics in a grid allows us to solve melodic problems by visually analyzing patterns.

EXERCISE

1. Write down the lyrics of a chorus with a repeating hook.

2. If there are lots of boxes with more than one syllable in them, grid in double-time. Write the chorus in the grid while tapping left to right and singing.

3. Identify patterns. Where are the hooks? Are they all aligned in the same boxes?

4. Replace the hook syllables with the notes of the hook melody and identify patterns. Does the hook melody match on every repetition? Does the melody surface anywhere else in the song?

CHAPTER 10
SOLVE AN EMPHASIS

After lyrics have been written, try reading them out loud, like a letter to a friend. Pay attention to the emphasis of each syllable. Lyrics are not conversation or poetry, where the speaker is in control of where the emphasis is placed. Whatever beat a syllable lands on determines whether it's emphasized. Ignoring this is the mark of an amateur.

Sometimes melody dictates the location of an emphasis, but usually it's the beat that has the most influence. Mostly the emphasis is going to be on a downbeat. In 4/4 time, the downbeat is the first of four beats.

The next example is Couldn't Walk Away, a song I wrote long ago. Back then, I wrote entirely by inspiration, before I ever thought about craft. Intuitively the song had a good story and hook, with clever internal rhymes and alliterations. But when I played it for a major publisher, he pinpointed a line with an emphasis issue. See if you can hear it.

LEARN THE SONG

For this example, we're only working on Verse 1.

<u>SONG</u>
COULDN'T WALK AWAY (Nomi Yah)

<u>LINE NUMBERS</u>
VERSE 1, LINE 1: I don't believe I was naïve
VERSE 1, LINE 2: When I believed our love was true
VERSE 1, LINE 3: But life is like a library
VERSE 1, LINE 4: You're always learning something new

VERSE 1, LINE 5: You did me wrong, I would be gone
VERSE 1, LINE 6: Considering what you put me through
VERSE 1, LINE 7: I made a choice and right or wrong
VERSE 1, LINE 8: Depends upon your point of view

<u>LISTEN</u>

YouTube Channel: Nomi Yah
Playlist: Writing Lyrics In A Grid
Song: Couldn't Walk Away
Link: https://youtu.be/ivm4KN6JhX8
Lyrics: Appendix 3, page 286

STEP 1

Did you hear the syllables that have the wrong emphasis in Verse 1, Line 3? If you did, congratulations, you have a good ear! When I wrote Couldn't Walk Away, I hadn't invented writing lyrics in a grid yet. If I had, I would have spotted the problem visually and spared myself the embarrassment of sounding like an amateur.

Use double-time to easily see the downbeat, in the first box of every row.

VERSE 1, LINE 1: I don't believe I was naïve
VERSE 1, LINE 2: When I believed our love was true
VERSE 1, LINE 3: But life is like a library
VERSE 1, LINE 4: You're always learning something new

Verse 1 (double-time):

x	x	x	I	don't	x	be	x
lieve	x	x	I	was	x	na	x
ive	x	x	when	I	x	be	x
lieved	x	x	our	love	x	was	x
true	x	x	but	life	x	is	x

184

like	x	x	a	li	x	bra	x
ry	x	x	you're	al	x	ways	x
learn	x	x	ing	some	x	thing	x
new							

STEP 2

Don't look for rhymes and variations in this example. Simply pay attention to the emphasis of syllables. The downbeat is usually emphasized, so focus on Boxes 1 of every row.

Verse 1 (double-time):

x	x	x	I	don't	x	be	x
lieve	x	x	I	was	x	na	x
ive	x	x	when	I	x	be	x
lieved	x	x	our	love	x	was	x
true	x	x	but	life	x	is	x
like	x	x	a	li	x	bra	x
ry	x	x	you're	al	x	ways	x
learn	x	x	ing	some	x	thing	x
new							

Check the pronunciation of each syllable in Boxes 1 by saying the word out loud.

Row 2, Box 1 "be-LIEVE" is correct.

Row 3, Box 1 "na-IVE" is correct.

Row 4, Box 1 "be-LIEVED" is correct.

Row 5, Box 1 "was TRUE" is correct.
Row 6, Box 1 "is LIKE" is incorrect. The word "like" is not emphasized in a sentence.

Row 7, Box 1 "li-bra-RY" is incorrect. It should be "LI-bra-ry".

Row 8, Box 1 "LEARN-ing" is correct.

Row 9, Box 1 "something NEW" is correct.

STEP 3

Verse 1 has a cool quadruple alliteration "life", "like", "library" and "learning". But there's an incorrect emphasis on two of the syllables and that's what irritated the trained ear of the publisher. The phrasing was so uniform, I didn't realize my pronunciation was off until the publisher commented on it.

Try saying it out loud. Emphasize the words that are capitalized. My version is "but life is LIKE a li-bra-RY". It doesn't sound right at all. It should be "but LIFE is like a LI-bra-ry".

Had I had penned Couldn't Walk Away after studying the fundamentals of songwriting, I would have rewritten the line to correct the emphasis issue. But it ended up on an album with the stray syllables. As it turned out, nobody other than that one publisher ever commented on it. But I cringe a little when I hear the recording and now you will too.

How might I have rewritten it to correct the emphasis? I could have moved each syllable that has an incorrect emphasis and that would have fixed the problem. I want it to say "but LIFE is like a LI-bra-ry". I'll start by putting "life" and "li" on the downbeats and changing the rest of the syllables to "dah".

Row 2, Box 1 = "life"
Row 3, Box 1 = "li"

Verse 1, Lines 3 & 4 (double-time):

			dah	dah	x	dah	x
life	x	x	dah	dah	x	dah	x
li	x	x	dah	dah	x	dah	x
learn	x	x	ing	some	x	thing	x
new							

Fill in the remainder of the word "library".

Row 3, Box 4 = "bra"
Row 3, Box 5 = "ry"

Verse 1, Lines 3 & 4 (double-time):

			dah	dah	x	dah	x
life	x	x	dah	dah	x	dah	x
li	x	x	bra	ry	x	dah	x
learn	x	x	ing	some	x	thing	x
new							

What comes after "library"? In the original version, it was "you're always learning something new". This no longer fits and I need to compress "you're always" from three syllables to one.

Row 3, Box 7 = "keep"

Verse 1, Lines 3 & 4 (double-time):

			dah	dah	x	dah	x
life	x	x	dah	dah	x	dah	x
li	x	x	bra	ry	x	keep	x
learn	x	x	ing	some	x	thing	x
new							

What comes before "library"? I want to keep the triple-alliteration "life", "like" and "library". Work backwards from "library".

Row 2, Box 7 = "a"
Row 2, Box 5 = "like"

Verse 1, Lines 3 & 4 (double-time):

			dah	dah	x	dah	x
life	x	x	dah	like	x	a	x
li	x	x	bra	ry	x	keep	x
learn	x	x	ing	some	x	thing	x
new							

What three syllables come before "life"? Before there was only one syllable "but" and now I'm going to extend it by adding two syllables to match the phrasing. Instead of the original "but life is like a library", I'm going to rewrite it "but this is life, it's like a library".

Row 1, Box 4 = "but"
Row 1, Box 5 = "this"
Row 1, Box 7 = "is"
Row 2, Box 4 = "it's"

Verse 1, Lines 3 & 4 (double-time):

			but	this	x	is	x
life	x	x	it's	like	x	a	x
li	x	x	bra	ry	x	keep	x
learn	x	x	ing	some	x	thing	x
new							

The rewrite sings "but this is LIFE, it's like a LI-bra-ry". Three of the four alliterations "life", "like", "library" and "learning" are emphasized, shining a spotlight on the alliteration.

The new version fixes the incorrect emphasis problems by slightly moving syllables in the grid.

STEP 4

The rewritten line doesn't change the lyrical content. It is a slight adjustment from:

> But life is like a library
> You're always learning something new

to:

> But this is life, it's like a library
> Keep learning something new.

This tiny alteration of phrasing significantly strengthens the song. Songwriters often can't discern a faint problem like this because we focus on the emotional impact of what we're conveying. It may be an unpleasant surprise when a lyric is critiqued as amateur, especially if we feel that the content is good.

The difference between amateur and great may be only a few syllables. Writing lyrics in a grid can take a song from almost-there to all-the-way-there.

SUMMARY

In Chapter 10, you learned how to:
- Solve an emphasis
- Find the emphasis of a word, usually on the downbeat
- Read lyrics out loud to make sure the emphasis of words is conversational

To write a well-crafted song, it's useful to speak the lyrics out loud. Make sure the emphasis of the syllables sound correct. If something isn't natural in spoken language, it will feel awkward in a song. Conversational lyrics work best to connect with a listener.

There are other issues in this verse. In Line 6, "considering" is pronounced "con-sid-er-ING". It should have been "con-SIDder-ing". In Line 8, "depends upon" is not conversational; "depending on" would have been a better choice. When I wrote the song, I didn't know how to solve an emphasis or a rhyme. If I had already invented writing lyrics in a grid this would have been a stronger song.

EXERCISE

1. Write down the verse of a song.

2. Create a grid.

3. Tap your finger from left to right and sing in time.

4. Write the lyrics in the grid.

5. Identify the syllables in the first box of each row. Say the line, emphasizing the syllable in the first box. Does it sound conversationally correct?

6. If any of the lines have an incorrect emphasis, rewrite it to correct the issue.

CHAPTER 11
WRITE FOR A PUBLISHER

When I hear a wonderful song, I write the lyrics in a grid to get to the bottom of what makes the song great. Writing lyrics in a grid is an educational tool that reveals the structure of a hit song. It's a boon for students of music appreciation.

Syllabalizing enables a deep understanding of songwriting, which is critical when writing for music publishers. It's a common scenario for publishers to give a few specific examples of the kind of material they're looking for. They want something original, not a copy but a tune that feels similar to the reference song. The new song wouldn't belong on the same album as the reference song but would be on the same playlist. The artist on the new song would play in the same concert as the reference artist but wouldn't be in the same band.

A common practice of professionals is to use a reference song as a template. Writing lyrics in a grid is an indispensable technique for this purpose. I'll show you how to write a similar song from a template by using my song Take A Day Off.

A publisher contacted me looking for an original song for a film. He requested the new song be similar to three well-known songs by three different artists. I used all three songs to create a template, ensuring the new song is similar but not an imitation.

I created the template with the verse from the first similar song, the chorus from the second, and the bridge from the third. Using three templates, instead of one, is a technique I call "triangulating".

Listen to the song and read the lyrics before we take it to the grid.

LEARN THE SONG

SONG
TAKE A DAY OFF (Nomi Yah)

LINE NUMBERS
VERSE 1, LINE 1: All that stuff you have to do now
VERSE 1, LINE 2: Can't it wait until tomorrow
VERSE 1, LINE 3: All we ever do is work
VERSE 1, LINE 4: Don't you think that we deserve
VERSE 1, LINE 5: An occasional time out
LIFT, LINE 1: We're going to be playing hooky, calling in sick
LIFT, LINE 2: Doing whatever we need to be together
CHORUS, LINE 1: Take a day, take a day, take a day off
CHORUS, LINE 2: It's time for getting in the sun
CHORUS, LINE 3: It's time for getting nothing done
CHORUS, LINE 4: Take a day, take a day, take a day off
CHORUS, LINE 5: We're going to finally get a break
CHORUS, LINE 6: We're going to finally get to take a day off
VERSE 2, LINE 1: Putting E&J in Pepsi
VERSE 2, LINE 2: Kicking it and getting tipsy
VERSE 2, LINE 3: We'll be acting juvenile
VERSE 2, LINE 4: Like it's going out of style
VERSE 2, LINE 5: I just love when you're with me
BRIDGE, LINE 1: I don't mean to make you delinquent
BRIDGE, LINE 2: But I want to say what I'm thinking

LISTEN
YouTube Channel: Nomi Yah
Playlist: Writing Lyrics In A Grid
Song: Take A Day Off
Link: https://youtu.be/eLV7gwE9hnM
Lyrics: Appendix 3, page 295

STEP 1

I don't have permissions to print the similar songs that the publisher gave me, but links to the songs are on the Writing Lyrics In A Grid playlist on YouTube.

LISTEN

YouTube Channel: Nomi Yah
Playlist: Writing Lyrics In A Grid
Song: Take A Bow
Link: https://youtu.be/J3UjJ4wKLkg

I'm using nonsense rhymes and syllables in place of the popular song lyrics. I'll grid the nonsense using the exact phrasing of the actual lyrics.

Similar Song #1 Verse:

x	x	dah	dah	dah	dah	dah	pop
x	x	x	x	x	x	x	x
x	x	dah	dah	dah	dah	dah	stop
x	x	x	x	x	x	x	x
dah	dah	dah	dah	dah	dah	pay	x
dah	dah	dah	dah	dah	dah	day	x
dah	x	x	dah	dah	x	dah	top

IDENTIFY PATTERNS

Similar Song #1 Verse:

x	x	dah	dah	dah	dah	dah	pop
x	x	x	x	x	x	x	x
x	x	dah	dah	dah	dah	dah	stop
x	x	x	x	x	x	x	x
dah	dah	dah	dah	dah	dah	pay	x
dah	dah	dah	dah	dah	dah	say	x

dah	x	x	dah	dah	x	dah	top

The patterns in this successful song are very repetitive.

Rows 1 and 3 match.

Rows 2 and 4 match.

Rows 5 and 6 match.

Rows 1, 3 and 7, Boxes 8 rhyme.

Rows 5 and 6, Boxes 7 rhyme.

STEP 2

Copy the pattern closely at first, but after a while change it up a bit, there's no need to be rigid. Leave room for creativity to allow the new song to be distinctly different from the similar song.

Begin with the template from Similar Song #1, created in the previous step.

Similar Song #1 Verse:

x	x	dah	dah	dah	dah	dah	pop
x	x	x	x	x	x	x	x
x	x	dah	dah	dah	dah	dah	stop
x	x	x	x	x	x	x	x
dah	dah	dah	dah	dah	dah	pay	x
dah	dah	dah	dah	dah	dah	day	x
dah	x	x	dah	dah	x	dah	top

Replace the nonsense with a story that makes sense.

New Verse 1:

x	x	all	that	stuff	you	have	to
do	x	now	x	x	x	x	x
x	x	can't	it	wait	un	til	to
mor	x	row	x	x	x	x	x
all	we	ev	er	do	is	work	x
don't	you	think	that	we	de	serve	x
x	x	an	oc	ca	sion	al	x
time	x	out					

New Verse 2:

x	x	put	ting	E	and	J	in
Pep	x	si	x	x	x	x	x
x	x	kick	ing	it	and	get	ting
tip	x	sy	x	x	x	x	x
we'll	be	act	ing	ju	ve	nile	x
like	it's	go	ing	out	of	style	x
x	x	I	just	love	when	you're	x
with	x	me					

The biggest variation from the similar song is in Rows 2, 4 and 8, Boxes 1 and 3, where the similar song is empty and the new song isn't.

The rhymes have the same pattern at the ends of lines 1, 2 and 5, but instead of being in Boxes 8, the near-rhymes are now in Boxes 3 "now", "row" and "out".

STEP 3

Similar Song #1 has a lift section in every verse, an extra two lines. I use the lift as a springboard and follow my inspiration in a different direction, matching Row 1 and changing up the rest of the section.

It's advisable to use the similar song as a guideline but not copy it too closely. We're creators, not imitators, and have to stay open to discovering our own nuggets of genius.

Similar Song #1 Lift:

dah	dah	dah	dah	dah	dah	dah	dah
dah	x	x	x	x	x	da da	da da
dah	dah	dah	dah	dah	dah	dah	dah
dah							

New Lift:

play	ing	hook	y	call	ing	in	sick
x	do	ing	what	ev	er	we	need
x	x	x	to	be	x	x	to
geth	x	er					

STEP 4

Moving on to the second similar song, syllabalize the chorus with nonsense syllables. The similar song has a long repetitive chorus and I'll only work with a third of the length. The catchy part of the similar song is the frequent repetition of the hook. For the hook, use the nonsense syllable "dibby" to mark where the hook lands. For all the other syllables, use "dah" as placeholders.

<u>LISTEN</u>

YouTube Channel: Nomi Yah
Playlist: Writing Lyrics In A Grid
Song: Baby
Link: https://youtu.be/kffacxfA7G4

Similar Song #2 Chorus:

						x dah	dah

dib	by	dib	by dib	x by	dah	x	dah
dib	by	dib	by dib	x by	dah	x	dah
dib	by	dib	by dib	x by	dah	x	dah
dah	dah	da da	dah	dah			

IDENTIFY PATTERNS

Similar Song #2 Chorus:

						x dah	dah
dib	by	dib	by dib	x by	dah	x	dah
dib	by	dib	by dib	x by	dah	x	dah
dib	by	dib	by dib	x by	dah	x	dah
dah	dah	da da	dah	dah			

The hook, with the nonsense placeholder "dibby", occurs nine times in this section. In the similar song, this section repeats. Commonly, a song repeats a hook three or four times in each chorus. In Similar Song #2, the hook repeats eighteen times in each chorus. Throughout the song, the hook occurs a whopping fifty-four times! The song is a huge hit and the repetitive hook is surely a primary reason.

STEP 5

Repeating the hook "dibby" eighteen times in each chorus is really excessive and I don't want to go that far. I'm going to repeat my hook "take a day" seven times in each chorus. It isn't as many times as in the similar song but still double the normal amount.

I write the chorus following the template, but once again I'm inspired to go a different direction. I'm not using the template at all, except the frequent repetition of the hook. Most of the chorus is written following my own creativity. The beauty of using similar song templates is the way it expands our palette.

Similar Song #2 Chorus:

						x dah	dah
dib	by	dib	by dib	x by	dah	x	dah
dib	by	dib	by dib	x by	dah	x	dah
dib	by	dib	by dib	x by	dah	x	dah
dah	dah	da da	dah	dah			

New Chorus:

						take	a
day	x	take	a	day	x	take	a
day	x	off	x	x	it's	time	for
get	ting in	x the	x sun	x	it's	time	for
get	ting noth	x ing	x done	x	x	take	a
day	x	take	a	day	x	take	a
day	x	off	x	x	we're	gon	na
fi	nally get	x a	x break	x	we're	gon	na
fi	nally get	x to	x take	x	x	x	a
day	x	off					

SUMMARY

In Chapter 11, you learned how to:
- Write for a publisher
- Use nonsense syllables and rhymes to create a template
- Triangulate by using three similar songs to build a template

To write a similar song, build a template and start by following it, replacing words. Then let your creativity wander off the template and go in your own direction. Following the template will make the new song sound like it's in the ballpark of the similar song. Veering off the template will make the new song original. Don't let templates induce plagiarism.

We could continue syllabalizing the bridge of Take A Day Off but you get the gist of it. Writing lyrics in a grid is an indispensable tool for dissecting and imitating a popular song. If you are a professional songwriter, this skill is invaluable.

EXERCISE

1. Pick three songs in the same genre. Write down the verse from the first song, the chorus from the second, and the bridge from the third.

2. Write the verse in the grid and identify patterns. Which lines match? Where are the rhymes? Create a template replacing rhymes with nonsense rhymes and other words with nonsense syllables.

3. Write new words with rhymes in the same places, replacing the nonsense rhymes with the new rhymes. Work backwards from the rhyme to fill in the new line.

4. Repeat the process with the rest of the song. Follow your creativity as it leads you away from the template.

5. Build a storyboard by summarizing each section in a single sentence. Read the sentences consecutively to see if the narrative is cohesive.

CHAPTER 12
WRITE A SIMILAR SONG

Write another similar song from a template using the familiar public domain lullaby Twinkle Twinkle. Since it's well-known, it will be easier to work on than the previous example, where I couldn't print the lyrics of the similar songs. Nonsense syllables make it harder to grasp the process.

In the obscure possibility you don't know or don't remember the lullaby, take a moment to listen and read the lyrics.

LEARN THE SONG

Most of the verses are unfamiliar. Focus only on the beloved first verse.

SONG
TWINKLE TWINKLE (Jane Taylor)

LINE NUMBERS
VERSE 1, LINE 1: Twinkle, twinkle, little star
VERSE 1, LINE 2: How I wonder what you are
VERSE 1, LINE 3: Up above the world so high
VERSE 1, LINE 4: Like a diamond in the sky
VERSE 1, LINE 5: Twinkle, twinkle, little star
VERSE 1, LINE 6: How I wonder what you are

LISTEN
YouTube Channel: Nomi Yah
Playlist: Writing Lyrics In A Grid
Song: Twinkle Twinkle

Link: https://youtu.be/K2e1wbaDiKc
Lyrics: Appendix 3, page 296

STEP 1

Even without a grid, you can hear the extremely repetitive style. It's the trademark of a lullaby, as we discussed in Chapter 4 with Mary Had A Little Lamb.

VERSE 1, LINE 1: Twinkle, twinkle, little star
VERSE 1, LINE 2: How I wonder what you are
VERSE 1, LINE 3: Up above the world so high
VERSE 1, LINE 4: Like a diamond in the sky
VERSE 1, LINE 5: Twinkle, twinkle, little star
VERSE 1, LINE 6: How I wonder what you are

Similar Song:

twin	kle	twin	kle	lit	tle	star	x
how	I	won	der	what	you	are	x
up	a	bove	the	world	so	high	x
like	a	dia	mond	in	the	sky	x
twin	kle	twin	kle	lit	tle	star	x
how	I	won	der	what	you	are	x

IDENTIFY PATTERNS

Similar Song:

twin	kle	twin	kle	lit	tle	star	x
how	I	won	der	what	you	are	x
up	a	bove	the	world	so	high	x
like	a	dia	mond	in	the	sky	x
twin	kle	twin	kle	lit	tle	star	x
how	I	won	der	what	you	are	x

We see the similarity to other lullabies. There's a predictable placement of syllables, repetitive and even.

Each line begins on a downbeat.

Every row has matching syllables.

The rhymes are at the end of consecutive lines, "star" and "are" and "high" and "sky".

Layers of simplicity form a song that even small children can easily learn.

STEP 2

Write a song on the spot, using Twinkle Twinkle as a template. We'll make something up to fit the phrasing, without worrying about meaning.

First, create a template. Start with the grid from Step 1.

Similar Song:

twin	kle	twin	kle	lit	tle	star	x
how	I	won	der	what	you	are	x
up	a	bove	the	world	so	high	x
like	a	dia	mond	in	the	sky	x
twin	kle	twin	kle	lit	tle	star	x
how	I	won	der	what	you	are	x

In Boxes 7, replace the rhymes with nonsense rhymes "pop" and "stop" and "shoe" and "glue".

Rows 1 and 5, Boxes 7 = "stop"
Rows 2 and 6, Boxes 7 = "pop"
Row 3, Box 7 = "shoe"

Row 4, Box 7 = "glue"

New Song:

twin	kle	twin	kle	lit	tle	stop	x
how	I	won	der	what	you	pop	x
up	a	bove	the	world	so	shoe	x
like	a	dia	mond	in	the	glue	x
twin	kle	twin	kle	lit	tle	stop	x
how	I	won	der	what	you	pop	x

Replace the other words with the nonsense syllable "dah".

New Song:

dah	dah	dah	dah	dah	dah	stop	x
dah	dah	dah	dah	dah	dah	pop	x
dah	dah	dah	dah	dah	dah	shoe	x
dah	dah	dah	dah	dah	dah	glue	x
dah	dah	dah	dah	dah	dah	stop	x
dah	dah	dah	dah	dah	dah	pop	x

STEP 3

I'm not going to wrestle with this and compose great lyrics, I just want to demonstrate how to use a template. Skip storyline and hook and just write random words.

Replace the syllables in Row 1.

LINE 1:   Sunny days and Ferris wheels

New Song:

sun	ny	days	and	Fer	ris	wheels	x
dah	dah	dah	dah	dah	dah	pop	x

210

dah	dah	dah	dah	dah	dah	shoe	x
dah	dah	dah	dah	dah	dah	glue	x
dah	dah	dah	dah	dah	dah	stop	x
dah	dah	dah	dah	dah	dah	pop	x

How can we rhyme "Ferris wheels"? First thing I think of is "apple peels".

Row 2, Box 7 = "peels"
Row 2, Box 6 = "ple"
Row 2, Box 5 = "ap"

New Song:

sun	ny	days	and	Fer	ris	wheels	x
dah	dah	dah	dah	ap	ple	peels	x
dah	dah	dah	dah	dah	dah	shoe	x
dah	dah	dah	dah	dah	dah	glue	x
dah	dah	dah	dah	dah	dah	stop	x
dah	dah	dah	dah	dah	dah	pop	x

How do we construct a sentence that ends in "apple peels"?

LINE 2:   Candy wrappers, apple peels

Row 2, Box 4 = "pers"
Row 2, Box 3 = "wrap"
Row 2, Box 2 = "dy"
Row 2, Box 1 = "can"

New Song:

sun	ny	days	and	Fer	ris	wheels	x
can	dy	wrap	pers	ap	ple	peels	x
dah	dah	dah	dah	dah	dah	shoe	x
dah	dah	dah	dah	dah	dah	glue	x
dah	dah	dah	dah	dah	dah	stop	x

dah	dah	dah	dah	dah	dah	pop	x

Here's a quick idea for the next pair of lines. Start with the rhyming words "fight" and "flight".

LINE 3:   Monkeys in a paintball fight
LINE 4:   Pair of pigeons taking flight

Row 3, Box 7 = "fight"
Row 4, Box 7 = "flight"

New Song:

sun	ny	days	and	Fer	ris	wheels	x
can	dy	wrap	pers	ap	ple	peels	x
dah	dah	dah	dah	dah	dah	fight	x
dah	dah	dah	dah	dah	dah	flight	x
dah	dah	dah	dah	dah	dah	stop	x
dah	dah	dah	dah	dah	dah	pop	x

Put the rest of the syllables in place, working backwards from the rhyme "fight" and "flight".

Row 3, Box 6 = "ball"
Row 3, Box 5 = "paint"
Row 3, Box 4 = "a"
Row 3, Box 3 = "in"
Row 3, Box 2 = "keys"
Row 3, Box 1 = "mon"
Row 4, Box 6 = "ing"
Row 4, Box 5 = "tak"
Row 4, Box 4 = "geons"
Row 4, Box 3 = "pi"
Row 4, Box 2 = "of"
Row 4, Box 1 = "pair"

New Song:

sun	ny	days	and	Fer	ris	wheels	x

can	dy	wrap	pers	ap	ple	peels	x
mon	keys	in	a	paint	ball	fight	x
pair	of	pi	geons	tak	ing	flight	x
dah	dah	dah	dah	dah	dah	stop	x
dah	dah	dah	dah	dah	dah	pop	x

One more couplet completes the verse. First put in the rhyming words "holiday" and "go away".

LINE 5:   We have had a holiday
LINE 6:   We'll pack up and go away

Row 5, Box 5 = "hol"
Row 5, Box 6 = "i"
Row 5, Box 7 = "day"
Row 6, Box 5 = "go"
Row 6, Box 6 = "a"
Row 6, Box 7 = "way"

New Song:

sun	ny	days	and	Fer	ris	wheels	x
can	dy	wrap	pers	ap	ple	peels	x
mon	keys	in	a	paint	ball	fight	x
pair	of	pi	geons	tak	ing	flight	x
dah	dah	dah	dah	hol	i	day	x
dah	dah	dah	dah	go	a	way	x

Work backwards from the rhymes to fill in the other syllables.

Row 5, Box 4 = "a"
Row 5, Box 3 = "had"
Row 5, Box 2 = "have"
Row 5, Box 1 = "we"
Row 6, Box 4 = "and"
Row 6, Box 3 = "up"
Row 6, Box 2 = "pack"

Row 6, Box 1 = "we'll"

New Song:

sun	ny	days	and	Fer	ris	wheels	x
can	dy	wrap	pers	ap	ple	peels	x
mon	keys	in	a	paint	ball	fight	x
pair	of	pi	geons	tak	ing	flight	x
we	have	had	a	hol	i	day	x
we'll	pack	up	and	go	a	way	x

Here's the finished verse:
    Sunny days and Ferris wheels
    Candy wrappers, apple peels
    Monkeys in a paintball fight
    Pair of pigeons taking flight
    We have had a holiday
    We'll pack up and go away

STEP 4

Try writing a completely different story, using the same template of Twinkle Twinkle from Step 2. Come up with something on the spot and don't worry about the meaning. Start with the rhyming words, then work backwards.

New Song #2:

dah	dah	dah	dah	dah	dah	stop	x
dah	dah	dah	dah	dah	dah	pop	x
dah	dah	dah	dah	dah	dah	shoe	x
dah	dah	dah	dah	dah	dah	glue	x
dah	dah	dah	dah	dah	dah	stop	x
dah	dah	dah	dah	dah	dah	pop	x

LINE 1:   Mommy baked a birthday cake

214

LINE 2:   It gave me a stomachache

Row 1, Box 5 = "birth"
Row 1, Box 6 = "day"
Row 1, Box 7 = "cake"
Row 2, Box 5 = "stom"
Row 2, Box 6 = "ach"
Row 2, Box 7 = "ache"

New Song #2:

dah	dah	dah	dah	birth	day	cake	x
dah	dah	dah	dah	stom	ach	ache	x
dah	dah	dah	dah	dah	dah	shoe	x
dah	dah	dah	dah	dah	dah	glue	x
dah	dah	dah	dah	dah	dah	stop	x
dah	dah	dah	dah	dah	dah	pop	x

Row 1, Box 4 = "a"
Row 1, Box 3 = "baked"
Row 1, Box 2 = "my"
Row 1, Box 1 = "mom"
Row 2, Box 4 = "a"
Row 2, Box 3 = "me"
Row 2, Box 2 = "gave"
Row 2, Box 1 = "it"

New Song #2:

Mom	my	baked	a	birth	day	cake	x
it	gave	me	a	stom	ach	ache	x
dah	dah	dah	dah	dah	dah	shoe	x
dah	dah	dah	dah	dah	dah	glue	x
dah	dah	dah	dah	dah	dah	stop	x
dah	dah	dah	dah	dah	dah	pop	x

LINE 3:   I would not have had so much
LINE 4:   If it wasn't good enough

Row 3, Box 5 = "had"
Row 3, Box 6 = "so"
Row 3, Box 7 = "much"
Row 4, Box 5 = "good"
Row 4, Box 6 = "e"
Row 4, Box 7 = "nough"

New Song #2:

Mom	my	baked	a	birth	day	cake	x
it	gave	me	a	stom	ach	ache	x
dah	dah	dah	dah	had	so	much	x
dah	dah	dah	dah	good	e	nough	x
dah	dah	dah	dah	dah	dah	stop	x
dah	dah	dah	dah	dah	dah	pop	x

Row 3, Box 4 = "have"
Row 3, Box 3 = "not"
Row 3, Box 2 = "would"
Row 3, Box 1 = "I"
Row 4, Box 4 = "n't"
Row 4, Box 3 = "was"
Row 4, Box 2 = "it"
Row 4, Box 1 = "if"

New Song #2:

Mom	my	baked	a	birth	day	cake	x
it	gave	me	a	stom	ach	ache	x
I	would	not	have	had	so	much	x
if	it	was	n't	good	e	nough	x
dah	dah	dah	dah	dah	dah	stop	x
dah	dah	dah	dah	dah	dah	pop	x

LINE 5:   Next time Mom gives me a treat
LINE 6:   I won't take so much to eat

Row 5, Box 7 = "treat"

216

Row 6, Box 7 = "eat"

New Song #2:

Mom	my	baked	a	birth	day	cake	x
it	gave	me	a	stom	ach	ache	x
I	would	not	have	had	so	much	x
if	it	was	n't	good	e	nough	x
dah	dah	dah	dah	dah	dah	treat	x
dah	dah	dah	dah	dah	dah	eat	x

Row 5, Box 6 = "a"
Row 5, Box 5 = "me"
Row 5, Box 4 = "gives"
Row 5, Box 3 = "mom"
Row 5, Box 2 = "time"
Row 5, Box 1 = "next"
Row 6, Box 6 = "to"
Row 6, Box 5 = "much"
Row 6, Box 4 = "so"
Row 6, Box 3 = "take"
Row 6, Box 2 = "won't"
Row 6, Box 1 = "I"

New Song #2:

Mom	my	baked	a	birth	day	cake	x
it	gave	me	a	stom	ach	ache	x
I	would	not	have	had	so	much	x
if	it	was	n't	good	e	nough	x
next	time	Mom	gives	me	a	treat	x
I	won't	take	so	much	to	eat	x

Here's the new song:
    Mommy baked a birthday cake
    It gave me a stomachache
    I would not have had so much
    If it wasn't good enough

Next time Mom gives me a treat
I won't take so much to eat

SUMMARY

In Chapter 12, you learned how to:
- Write a similar song
- Compare patterns and syllabalize

The lullaby pattern is memorable and easy. Twinkle Twinkle has the same melody as The ABC, the song used to teach the alphabet to young children, and Baa Baa Black Sheep. The melody was popular long before Mozart put his name on the composition.

Using templates is a great way to brainstorm. There's no limit to the possibilities. Writing lyrics in a grid is an effective method to write from the template of a similar song.

EXERCISE

1. Write the lyrics of a lullaby in the grid and identify patterns. Which lines match? Where are the rhymes?

2. Create a template by replacing the rhymes with nonsense rhymes and replacing the other words with nonsense syllables.

3. Write new words with rhymes in the same places. Replace the nonsense rhymes with the new rhymes.
4. Work backwards from the rhymes to fill in the new lines.

5. Using the same template, start over with new words and write another song. This is such a valuable technique, it's worth repeating.

CHAPTER 13
WRITE FOR AN ARTIST

In a previous chapter, we used syllabalization to write for a publisher. The publishers knew what kind of song they wanted and we gave them a similar song by using a template. In this chapter, we'll use a grid to write for an artist. The artist has an unfinished idea that needs to be thoroughly understood and mimicked. That's the only way to make a song sound like the singer wrote it. Writing lyrics in a grid is the most accurate method to achieve this.

Using syllabalization to write for an artist has been responsible for a significant portion of my music income. While it takes a great deal of work to be a good performer, it's a different skill set to be a competent writer. Contrary to popular belief, most singers are not songwriters, just as most actors are not scriptwriters. That's where I come in, because a great song doesn't happen by itself.

Picture this, my phone rang at three in the morning, waking me from a deep sleep. It was a cowriter, saying she'd been partying at a club and was calling from an all-night diner near my house. She wanted to introduce me to a producer from Aftermath Entertainment, who had driven up from L.A. to visit the Bay. The owner of the label was Dr. Dre, one of my favorite music producers.

My friend handed the phone over to the producer, who said he heard I'm a good lyricist. He was shopping for songs for a young artist, who had just been signed to the label, and asked if I could sing one of my songs for him. I was in bed half-asleep, but the music industry doesn't have business hours. I didn't hesitate and started singing one of my songs into the phone. He was impressed and asked if I could have a song ready for him by

10:00 a.m. the following morning. He was leaving back to L.A. and would listen to my music on the drive home.

I leapt out of bed, threw on clothes, and went out into the cold night. I met them at the diner and the producer handed me a CD with three rough tracks. He said I could write a topline to any of the tunes and record a scratch vocal right on top of the draft track. He and my friend urged me to join them but I declined. I had no time to waste socializing, I hurried home and went to work. I wanted to write three songs, one for each track, to give me better odds of getting a deal. Regardless of time constraints, I was always an over-writer.

The tracks had sparse instrumentation, the sketch of hit songs. The young artist was singing meaningless sentence fragments. But his vocal tone was exceptional and there was a definitive it-factor charisma in his performance. There was no storyline, but the rhythm of his voice sounded cool. He had a great sense of style and a knack for melody. In terms of the songwriting elements,

1. Music
2. Hook
3. Melody
4. Words
5. Story

this artist only did melody. But often talent, youth and good looks are sufficient for a record deal. Since he was an excellent performer, he didn't have to be a competent writer.

I wanted to make sure the singer would like my songs and choose them for his debut album. For this reason, I stuck tightly to his phrasing, to accurately write in his style.

When writing for a publisher, as in a previous chapter, the new song has to be different from the similar song. We use the template as a starting point to maintain similarity, then branch off in new directions to avoid imitating. But when we're writing for an artist, it's better to follow their phrasing and not our own.

To follow the artist's phrasing, I gridded his singing, carefully putting each one of the mumbled syllables in the precise box that corresponded with his rhythm. Then I replaced each syllable with words making sense in a narrative.

Beginning with story, as is my tendency, I brainstormed a concept: a man caught his girlfriend cheating, on the very same day he was planning to propose to her. I sang along with the artist to get a first draft that would fit his style, then I syllabalized to make it accurate. The first draft ended up in a verse.

> Just this morning I asked you
> To go out tonight on a date
> Told you to get dressed special
> But I got slapped by the hand of fate

I wrote and recorded three songs in six hours, finishing in time to meet the producer and hand him a CD. Later the same evening, he called to offer me a contract for all three songs and that's how I got signed to Aftermath.

Writing and recording three songs in one night isn't how I work. I prefer to let a song grow in its own time. It could take a day or a decade to complete, that doesn't matter to me. I've never been impressed by songwriters who brag about writing quickly. But my writing preferences went out the window when it was Aftermath calling!

Writing lyrics in a grid is the critical tool that enabled me to crank out three songs in the unique style of an unfamiliar artist. Years of daily writing came into play, but the grid gave me the edge that got those songs signed to a major label.

Six months later, the artist was dropped from Aftermath and the record would never be released. I don't know the reason they discontinued the project, but it's the kind of thing that happens all the time. What I do know is my material reverted back to me. Before signing a song contract, check for a reversion clause. This can prevent your work from being eternally shelved.

LEARN THE SONG

The songs I wrote for Aftermath were never released, but I still have the original songwriter demo I gave to the producer. It isn't a finished version at all, it's just a middle-of-the-night sketch for the producer and artist to build on. I'm a woman singing a man's song, so please use your imagination. Listen closely and you'll hear the artist and record producer in the background.

Only work on the second verse, not the whole song. Once you understand the process, it's the same for the rest of it.

<u>SONG</u>
SLIDE (Nomi Yah)

<u>LINE NUMBERS</u>
VERSE 2, LINE 1: Just this morning I asked you
VERSE 2, LINE 2: To go out tonight on a date
VERSE 2, LINE 3: Told you to get dressed special
VERSE 2, LINE 4: But I got slapped by the hand of fate
VERSE 2, LINE 5: So, I had to cancel the reservations
VERSE 2, LINE 6: The same place my own father proposed
VERSE 2, LINE 7: Had to go back and return the diamonds
VERSE 2, LINE 8: I had to toss out a dozen roses

<u>ARTIST DRAFT LINE NUMBERS</u>
VERSE 2, LINE 1: Girl, you making me crazy
VERSE 2, LINE 2: And you get what you gonna take
VERSE 2, LINE 3: Gonna be going crazy
VERSE 2, LINE 4: But girl you know what I'm gonna say

VERSE 2, LINE 5: Sipping on a Henny and getting crazy
VERSE 2, LINE 6: And it'll be baby girl you be you know
VERSE 2, LINE 7: Girl you don't know well you got up and do it
VERSE 2, LINE 8: Girl, you will never know it you know

LISTEN

YouTube Channel:	Nomi Yah
Playlist:	Writing Lyrics In A Grid
Song:	Slide
Link:	https://youtu.be/5U27lMXZowM
Lyrics:	Appendix 3, page 294

STEP 1

Make the new draft fit the phrasing of the artist. Put his improvisation in a grid. He's mumbling but we can follow his rhythms.

Begin with the odd numbered lines. Double-time works best to handle the syncopated lyrics.

ARTIST DRAFT VERSE 1, LINE 1: Girl, you making me crazy

Artist Draft (double-time):

girl	x	you	x	mak	ing	x	me
cra	x	zy					

ARTIST DRAFT VERSE 1, LINE 3: Gonna be going crazy

Artist Draft Verse 1, Line 3 (double-time):

gon	x	na	x be	go	x	ing	x
cra	x	zy					

IDENTIFY PATTERNS

Break Lines 1 and 3 into separate grids to see the patterns more easily.

Artist Draft Verse 1, Line 1 (double-time):

girl	x	you	x	mak	ing	x	me
cra	x	zy					

Artist Draft Verse 1, Line 3 (double-time):

gon	x	na	<u>x be</u>	go	x	ing	x
cra	x	zy					

Rows 1, Boxes 4 have a variation. Verse 1, Line 1 is empty "x". Verse 1, Line 3 has a space "x" and a syllable "be" in one box.

Rows 1, Boxes 6 have a variation, with Verse 1, Line 1 having an extra syllable "ing".

Rows 1, Boxes 7 have a variation, with Verse 1, Line 3 having an extra syllable "ing".

Rows 1, Boxes 8 have a variation, with Verse 1, Line 3 having an extra syllable "me".

Rows 2 are identical, with both lines having the word "crazy" in the same place.

Laid out in a grid, it's obvious the artist was improvising. He made no attempt at repetition or rhyme. But there is a nugget embedded in the draft. The artist has an undeniable instinct of rhythm that is his untamed natural state. If I impose a more rigid style, he might not feel right performing it.

I'll spurn songwriting conventions this time and write lyrics matching his sporadic phrasing as closely as possible. I don't know the artist personally and I'd rather be right in his pocket than challenge his style. Sometimes it isn't what you say that matters, it's how you say it, especially when it comes to the style of an artist.

STEP 2

Put Verse 1, Lines 1 and 3 back on a single grid. Write new lyrics in a separate grid, copying the phrasing precisely from the artist draft.

Artist Draft Verse 1, Lines 1 & 3 (double-time):

girl	x	you	x	mak	ing	x	me
cra	x	zy					
gon	x	na	x be	go	x	ing	x
cra	x	zy					

VERSE 1, LINE 1: Just this morning I asked you
VERSE 1, LINE 3: Told you to get dressed special

New Verse 1, Lines 1 & 3 (double-time):

just	x	this	x	morn	ing	x	I
asked	x	you					
told	x	you	x to	get	x	dressed	x
spe	x	cial					

My urge is to make Lines 1 and 3 the same, a common songwriting form. But here I follow the artist's variations precisely. The only thing I want to change is the story.

Can I write something more carefully crafted, rather than following the artist's improvisation? Sure, I can, and it would be objectively better. But I'm betting I'll have more success if the song mirrors the artist, making him feel like it's his own creation. I stick closely to his patterns.

STEP 3

The odd verse lines were completed in the previous step. Next repeat the process for the even lines. Create a template for the even lines by laying out the artist's phrasing in the grid. Then write lyrics in the same boxes as his syllables.

ARTIST DRAFT VERSE 1, LINE 2: And you get what you gonna take

Artist Draft Verse 1, Line 2 (double-time):

						and	you
get	x	what	you	x	gon	x	na
take							

ARTIST DRAFT VERSE 1, LINE 4: But girl you know what I'm gonna say

Artist Draft Verse 1, Line 4 (double-time):

					but	girl	you
know	what	x	I'm	gon	na	x	x
say							

<u>IDENTIFY PATTERNS</u>

Artist Draft Verse 1, Line 2 (double-time):

						and	you
get	x	what	you	x	gon	x	na
take							

Artist Draft Verse 1, Line 4 (double-time):

					but	girl	you
know	what	x	I'm	gon	na	x	x
say							

Rows 1, Boxes 6 have a variation, with Verse 1, Line 4 having an extra syllable "but".

Rows 2, Boxes 2 have a variation, with Verse 1, Line 4 having an extra syllable "what".

Rows 2, Boxes 3 have a variation, with Verse 1, Line 2 having an extra syllable "what".

Rows 2, Boxes 5 have a variation, with Verse 1, Line 4 having an extra syllable "but".

Rows 2, Boxes 8 have a variation, with Verse 1, Line 2 having an extra syllable "na".

Rows 3, Boxes 1 have a near rhyme "take" and "say".

The artist is clearly not using repetition and variation in a conscious way. The syllables are haphazardly placed, but I'm going to follow them anyway to stay in the pocket of the artist's style.

STEP 4

Put the artist draft and the new grid together. Make the phrasing and rhyme scheme match. By writing the lyrics in a grid, we precisely follow the artist's phrasing, with all his unintentional variations.

Artist Draft Verse 1, Lines 2 & 4 (double-time):

							and	you
get	x	what	you	x	gon	x	na	
take								
						but	girl	you
know	what	x	I'm	gon	na	x	x	
say								

VERSE 1, LINE 2: To go out tonight on a date
VERSE 1, LINE 4: But I got slapped by the hand of fate

New Verse 1, Lines 2 & 4 (double-time):

							to	go
out	x	to	night	x	on	x	a	
date								
						but	I	got
slapped	by	x	the	hand	of	x	x	
fate								

STEP 5

Put the odd and even lines together and look at the verse as a whole. Put together on one page, you'll notice how relentlessly I stick to the artist's patterns. All I do is replace his nonsense with an actual story.

Artist Draft Verse 1 (double-time):

girl	x	you	x	mak	ing	x	me
cra	x	zy	x	x	x	and	you
get	x	what	you	x	gon	x	na
take	x	x	x	x	x	x	x
gon	x	na	x be	go	x	ing	x
cra	x	zy	x	x	but	girl	you
know	what	x	I'm	gon	na	x	x
say							

New Verse 1 (double-time):

just	x	this	x	morn	ing	x	I
asked	x	you	x	x	x	to	go
out	x	to	night	x	on	x	a
date	x	x	x	x	x	x	x
told	x	you	x to	get	x	dressed	x
spe	x	cial	x	x	but	I	got
slapped	by	x	the	hand	of	x	x
fate							

SUMMARY

In Chapter 13, you learned how to:
- Write for an artist
- Create a template from an artist draft

To write for an artist, closely follow their style, replacing their nonsense with a cohesive storyline. I've done this countless times, often receiving desperate calls asking me to resolve lyric emergencies. The artist is in the vocal booth, where talent and improvisation are not enough. They need a strong song before too much expensive studio time accumulates.

These kind of situations create an opening for a songwriter who is prepared to write on the spot and adapt to an artist's style. Writing lyrics in a grid simplifies the process. You're able to confidently rise to the occasion when an opportunity presents itself.

EXERCISE

1. Write down the verse of a song in a style you don't normally listen to.

2. Write the lyrics in the grid and identify patterns. Which lines match? Where are the variations? Where are the rhymes?

3. Create a template by replacing the rhymes with nonsense rhymes and replacing the other words with nonsense syllables.

4. Write a new line.

5. Replace the nonsense rhymes with the new rhymes.

6. Work backwards from the rhymes to fill in the new words, replacing the nonsense syllables.

7. Write another line that rhymes with the first.

8. Replace the rhyming word first, then work backwards to fill in the new sentence, replacing the nonsense syllables.

CHAPTER 14
SYLLABALIZE IN ALTERNATE TIME

The most common time signature is 4/4, with four beats in a bar. The second most frequently heard time signature is 3/4, with three beats in a bar.

Writing lyrics in a grid in 3/4 time is the same as in 4/4. The only thing that changes is the grid itself. The number of columns correspond to the number of beats in a bar. In 4/4, we use eight columns, while in 3/4, we use six columns. (For how to construct a six-column grid, refer to Chapter 3.)

A well-known nursery rhyme in 3/4 time is Row Row Row. We'll syllabalize in the alternate time signature.

LEARN THE SONG

It's very likely you know this song but here is a reminder. There's only one verse, it won't take long.

SONG
ROW, ROW, ROW (Eliphalet Oram Lyte)

LINE NUMBERS
LINE 1: Row, row, row your boat
LINE 2: Gently down the stream
LINE 3: Merrily, merrily, merrily, merrily
LINE 4: Life is but a dream

YouTube Channel:	Nomi Yah
Playlist:	Writing Lyrics In A Grid
Song:	Row Row Row
Link:	https://youtu.be/NYHvuN273do
Lyrics:	Appendix 3, page 292

STEP I

In the same way as before, tap your finger in the boxes from left to right while singing and fill in the boxes with syllables.

LINE 1: Row, row, row, your boat

Row 1, Box 1 = "row"
Row 1, Box 2 and 3 = "x"
Row 1, Box 4 = "row"
Row 1, Box 5 and 6 = "x"

row	x	x	row	x	x

Row 2, Box 1 = "row"
Row 2, Box 2 = "x"
Row 2, Box 3 = "your"
Row 2, Box 4 = "boat"

row	x	x	row	x	x
row	x	your	boat		

STEP 2

Fill in the rest of the lines in the same way as Line 1.

LINE 2: Gently down the stream

240

Row 2, Boxes 5 and 6 = "x"
Row 3, Box 1 = "gent"
Row 3, Box 2 = "x"
Row 3, Box 3 = "ly"
Row 3, Box 4 = "down"
Row 3, Box 5 = "x"
Row 3, Box 6 = "the"
Row 4, Box 1 = "stream"

row	x	x	row	x	x
row	x	your	boat	x	x
gent	x	ly	down	x	the
stream					

LINE 3: Merrily, merrily, merrily, merrily

Row 4, Boxes 2, 3, 4, 5 and 6 = "x"
Rows 5 and 6, Boxes 1 = "mer"
Rows 5 and 6, Boxes 2 = "ri"
Rows 5 and 6, Boxes 3 = "ly"
Rows 5 and 6, Boxes 4 = "mer"
Rows 5 and 6, Boxes 5 = "ri"
Rows 5 and 6, Boxes 6 = "ly"

row	x	x	row	x	x
row	x	your	boat	x	x
gent	x	ly	down	x	the
stream	x	x	x	x	x
mer	ri	ly	mer	ri	ly
mer	ri	ly	mer	ri	ly

LINE 4: Life is but a dream

Row 7, Box 1 = "life"
Row 7, Box 2 = "x"
Row 7, Box 3 = "is"

Row 7, Box 4 = "but"
Row 7, Box 5 = "x"
Row 7, Box 6 = "a"
Row 8, Box 1 = "dream"

row	x	x	row	x	x
row	x	your	boat	x	x
gent	x	ly	down	x	the
stream	x	x	x	x	x
mer	ri	ly	mer	ri	ly
mer	ri	ly	mer	ri	ly
life	x	is	but	x	a
dream					

IDENTIFY PATTERNS

row	x	x	row	x	x
row	x	your	boat	x	x
gent	x	ly	down	x	the
stream	x	x	x	x	x
mer	ri	ly	mer	ri	ly
mer	ri	ly	mer	ri	ly
life	x	is	but	x	a
dream					

Boxes 1 and 4 have most of the syllables. This emphasizes the first of every three beats. The emphasis on downbeats is familiar, the simplicity of a lullaby.

SUMMARY

In Chapter 14, you learned how to:
* Syllabalize in alternate time

Syllabalizing works the same way in any time signature. As long as the number of columns match the number of beats, the process is simple. Syllabalizing in alternate time is as simple as in 4/4.

Here are some other examples of lyrics in alternate time.

LISTEN

YouTube Channel:	Nomi Yah
Playlist:	Writing Lyrics In A Grid
Song:	My Country 'Tis Of Thee
Link:	https://youtu.be/VKj7FLg3WVA
Lyrics:	Appendix 3, page 289

My Country 'Tis Of Thee (Samuel Francis Smith)

my	coun	try	'tis	x of	thee
sweet	land	of	li	x ber	ty
of	thee	I	sing	x	x
land	where	my	fa	x thers	died
land	of	the	pil	x grims	pride
from	ev	very	moun	x tain	side
let	free	dom	ring	x	x

LISTEN

YouTube Channel:	Nomi Yah
Playlist:	Writing Lyrics In A Grid
Song:	Rock-A-Bye Baby
Link:	https://youtu.be/nuVVwZjLnf0
Lyrics:	Appendix 3, page 292

Rock-A-Bye Baby (Mother Goose)

rock	x a	bye	ba	x	by
in	x the	tree	top	x	x

when	x the	wind	blows	x	the
cra	dle	will	rock	x	x
when	x the	bough	breaks	x	the
cra	dle	will	fall	x	and
down	will	come	ba	x	by
cra	dle	and	all	x	x

LISTEN

YouTube Channel:　Nomi Yah
Playlist:　　　　　Writing Lyrics In A Grid
Song:　　　　　　Happy Birthday
Link:　　　　　　https://youtu.be/WEgG-Qhc1iQ
Lyrics:　　　　　Appendix 3, page 287

Happy Birthday (Patty Hill, Mildred J Hill)

			hap	x	py
birth	x	x	day	x	x
to	x	x	you	x	x
x	x	x	hap	x	py
birth	x	x	day	x	x
to	x	x	you	x	x
x	x	x	hap	x	py
birth	x	x	day	x	hap
py	x	x	birth	x	x
day	x	x	hap	x	py
birth	x	x	day	x	x
to	x	x	you		

EXERCISE

1. Write the lyrics of a song in ¾ time.

2. Write the syllables in the grid

3. Identify patterns.

CHAPTER 15
SYLLABALIZE A CHICKEN

The melody of birds has inspired centuries of composers. I've applied bird melody to writing lyrics in a grid. It works with any bird, really anything making a sound.

I've never experienced writer's block, but apparently listening to birds has helped many a songwriter overcome this obstacle.

Sometimes I hear a small nondescript bird in my yard, singing for an hour straight without repeating a pattern. When I take time to listen, the variations are astonishing. But we'll use a simpler bird in this chapter, my backyard chicken.

STEP 1

When my chicken is happily pecking and scratching, she clucks in a specific pattern. It's fairly repetitive and I'll syllabalize her rhythm as closely as I can.

Chicken Verse:

bah	x	buk	buk	buk	x	buk	buk
bah	x	buk	buk	buk			

Repeat the pattern to create a simple four-line verse.

Chicken Verse:

bah	x	buk	buk	buk	x	buk	buk
bah	x	buk	buk	buk			
bah	x	buk	buk	buk	x	buk	buk
bah	x	buk	buk	buk			

STEP 2

Write lyrics for the first line, following the pattern of the chicken template. Don't worry about meaning, just come up with something.

Chicken Verse:

bah	x	buk	buk	buk	x	buk	buk
bah	x	buk	buk	buk			
bah	x	buk	buk	buk	x	buk	buk
bah	x	buk	buk	buk			

LINE 1:   Why don't we see eye to eye anymore

New Verse:

why	x	don't	we	see	x	eye	to
eye	x	an	y	more			
bah	x	buk	buk	buk	x	buk	buk
bah	x	buk	buk	buk			

IDENTIFY PATTERNS

New Verse:

why	x	don't	we	see	x	eye	to
eye	x	an	y	more			
bah	x	buk	buk	buk	x	buk	buk
bah	x	buk	buk	buk			

Row 2, Box 5 "more" should rhyme in Row 4, Box 5.

Row 1, Box 5 "see" could have an internal rhyme in Row 3, Box 5.

Row 1, Box 1 "why" rhymes with Row 2, Box 1 "eye". The internal rhyme could repeat in Rows 3 and 4, Boxes 1.

250

STEP 3

We noted internal and external rhymes we could add in the previous step. Put nonsense rhymes in those places.

Row 4, Box 5 = "poor"
Row 3, Box 5 = "dee"
Row 3, Box 1 = "dye"
Row 4, Box 1 = "pie"

New Verse:

why	x	don't	we	see	x	eye	to
eye	x	an	y	more			
dye	x	buk	buk	dee	x	buk	buk
pie	x	buk	buk	poor			

In this step, find a rhyme for "more". There are many choices in a rhyming dictionary, including door, floor, roar, pour, shore, explore, ignore, restore, adore.

I'm going to use core because it's uncommon to hear that word in a song. It may be overused in gyms, but not in lyrics.

Row 4, Box 5 is "core".

New Verse:

why	x	don't	we	see	x	eye	to
eye	x	an	y	more			
dye	x	buk	buk	dee	x	buk	buk
pie	x	buk	buk	core			

Make the rhyme more conversational "to the core". Work backwards from the rhyme to solve for it.

Row 4, Box 4 = "the"
Row 4, Box 3 = "to"

New Verse:

why	x	don't	we	see	x	eye	to
eye	x	an	y	more			
dye	x	buk	buk	dee	x	buk	buk
pie	x	to	the	core			

STEP 4

"See" can have an internal rhyme in Row 3, Box 5. It's one of the easiest words to rhyme. I like the near rhyme "deep" because the meaning is in the realm of "core". This helps the lyrics stay focused on the story.

Row 3, Box 5 = "deep"

New Verse:

why	x	don't	we	see	x	eye	to
eye	x	an	y	more			
dye	x	buk	buk	deep	x	buk	buk
pie	x	to	the	core			

How can the words "deep" and "to the core" fit into a single sentence? Write a sentence that works for both rhymes and also fits the chicken syllables. Try "I'm breathing deep and I'm cut to the core". Row 4, Box 1 doesn't have the internal rhyme, but I'm going to allow it. Solve for the rhyme, working backwards.

LINE 2:   I'm breathing deep and I'm cut to the core

Row 4, Box 2 = "x"
Row 4, Box 1 = "cut"
Row 3, Box 8 = "I'm"
Row 3, Box 7 = "and"
Row 3, Box 4 = "ing"
Row 3, Box 3 = "breath"

Row 3, Box 1 = "I'm"

New Verse:

why	x	don't	we	see	x	eye	to
eye	x	an	y	more			
I'm	x	breath	ing	deep	x	and	I'm
cut	x	to	the	core			

STEP 5

When my chicken lays an egg, she always sounds the same way. It's a loud squawking, like a big diva chorus.

Chicken Chorus:

buk	buk	buk	buk	bah	x	x	buk
buk	buk	buk	buk	bah			

Let's double it to make a full-sized chorus.

Chicken Chorus:

buk	buk	buk	buk	bah	x	x	buk
buk	buk	buk	buk	bah	x	x	x
buk	buk	buk	buk	bah	x	x	buk
buk	buk	buk	buk	bah			

Come up with words fitting the patterns. Begin with the first row.

LINE 1:   Go on pack your crap

Row 1, Box 1 = "go"
Row 1, Box 2 = "on"
Row 1, Box 3 = "pack"
Row 1, Box 4 = "your"

Row 1, Box 5 = "crap"

New Chorus:

go	on	pack	your	crap	x	x	buk
buk	buk	buk	buk	bah	x	x	x
buk	buk	buk	buk	bah	x	x	buk
buk	buk	buk	buk	bah			

Row 1, Box 5 "crap" could rhyme in Row 3, Box 5. Use the nonsense syllable "dap".

Row 3, Box 5 = "dap"

New Chorus:

go	on	pack	your	crap	x	x	buk
buk	buk	buk	buk	bah	x	x	x
buk	buk	buk	buk	dap	x	x	buk
buk	buk	buk	buk	bah			

STEP 6

The next line has six syllables. How about "goodbye and adios"? It sounds like a hook, so let's repeat it in Line 4.

LINE 2:   Goodbye and adios
LINE 4:   Goodbye and adios

Rows 1 and 3, Box 8 = "good"
Rows 2 and 4, Box 1 = "bye"
Rows 2 and 4, Box 2 = "and"
Rows 2 and 4, Box 3 = "a"
Rows 2 and 4, Box 4 = "di"
Rows 2 and 4, Box 5 = "os"

New Chorus:

go	on	pack	your	crap	x	x	good
bye	and	a	di	os	x	x	x
buk	buk	buk	buk	dap	x	x	good
bye	and	a	di	os			

STEP 7

In the previous step, we noted Row 1, Box 5 "crap" should have a rhyme. How about the near rhyme "back"?

Row 3, Box 5 = "back"

New Chorus:

go	on	pack	your	crap	x	x	good
bye	and	a	di	os	x	x	x
buk	buk	buk	buk	back	x	x	good
bye	and	a	di	os			

There are four more chicken syllables left in Row 3, before "back". We could try "never looking back". Work backwards and solve the rhyme.

LINE 3:   Never looking back

Row 3, Box 4 = "ing"
Row 3, Box 3 = "look"
Row 3, Box 2 = "er"
Row 3, Box 1 = "nev"

Chorus:

go	on	pack	your	crap	x	x	good
bye	and	a	di	os	x	x	x
nev	er	look	ing	back	x	x	good

bye	and	a	di	os	x	x	

SUMMARY

In Chapter 15, you learned how to:
- Syllabalize a bird
- Listen to birds to eliminate writer's block

We syllabalized a chicken. It's a rough first draft of a verse and chorus idea. We could develop it into a full-blown song.

This isn't just for the birds. When we open our ears and listen to every sound equally, interesting melodies and words emerge.

It's easy to find inspiration. Goodbye and adios to writer's block.

GOODBYE AND ADIOS

Why don't we see
Eye to eye anymore
I'm breathing deep
And I'm cut to the core

Go on pack your crap
Goodbye and adios
Never looking back
Goodbye and adios

New Song:

why	x	don't	we	see	x	eye	to
eye	x	an	y	more	x	x	x
I'm	x	breath	ing	deep	x	and	I'm
cut	x	to	the	core	x	x	x
go	on	pack	your	crap	x	x	good
bye	and	a	di	os	x	x	x

nev	er	look	ing	back	x	x	good
bye	and	a	di	os			

EXERCISE

1. Go outside. Be silent. Listen to birds. Learn one of the bird melodies, find something you can hum to yourself. Sing the bird melody while tapping left to right. Write nonsense syllables in the grid in the correct boxes. Repeat the pattern to create two lines.

2. Replace the first line with words that make sense and fit into the pattern.

3. Find a word that rhymes with the end of the first line. Write the second rhyme in same box number as the first rhyme, but in a different row. Work backwards from the second rhyme to fill in the rest of the line.

4. Identify patterns. Are the two lines the same or are there variations? Does the new story make sense or do you want to add some lines to further expound?

5. Instead of a bird melody, try this exercise with a snippet of overheard conversation.

CHAPTER 16
CONCLUSION AND BONUS TIPS

Writing lyrics in a grid is a visual way to identify a lyrical problem and pop the words into alignment. This is the first songwriting technique using your eyes, not just your ears.

I was going for simplicity when I designed the method of writing lyrics in a grid. It's meant to be extremely easy to use. While it isn't difficult, it does require a great deal of detailed explaining to convey the concept. I sincerely hope you were able to understand, and if anything was confusing, I humbly request feedback. Your suggestions will be helpful for future revisions.

LESSONS LEARNED

After decades in hiding, I'm finally revealing my secret. I thoroughly taught you my method, with painstaking granular precision.

This book taught you how to:
- Add prosody to increase lyrical depth
- Compare patterns
- Compensate for a non-vertical hook
- Count to eight on one or two hands
- Create a template with nonsense syllables
- Identify patterns
- Make grids
- Put a reversion clause in a contract
- Recognize patterns of a lullaby
- Recognize songwriting tendencies
- Solve a melody
- Solve a rhyme by working backwards

- Solve an emphasis
- Syllabalize a bird
- Syllabalize in alternate time
- Syllabalize in double-time
- Triangulate using three songs to build a template
- Understand five elements of song composition
- Use a grid to polish a rough draft
- Use a grid to write from scratch
- Use symbols
- Write for a publisher
- Write for an artist
- Write syllables in a grid

BONUS TIPS

In addition to teaching you how to write lyrics in a grid, I'll take this opportunity to include some additional random tips about practicing, performing and songwriting.

PRACTICING TIPS

You can fit in extra practice time while driving to a show. Listen to a recording, or a song in your mind, and "play along" by pressing your fingers into the steering wheel, or the dashboard if you're in the passenger seat. Form correct chords and notes. You'll learn the song nearly as well as if you were playing an instrument.

To learn a song in the shortest time, don't play the song from beginning to end, over and over. Learn the sections separately and then work on transitions. For example, zero in on the transition going from a verse into a chorus, and just practice those few bars. To sound more polished, always work on the very beginning and ending of a song. Focusing on transitions is especially helpful in getting the most out of limited practice time. It's a good way for a bandleader to herd spacy musician cats.

Think of practice as two separate activities, Technical and Performance. During Technical Practice, don't play the entire song. The goal is to work only on places that need improvement, to fine-tune rough spots. But during Performance Practice, play the entire song, or whole set, with no pause. In Performance Practice, the goal is to be transported by the music, not thinking about technical details.

The reason professionals don't have "a bad night" is because they practice having charisma on tap. Record every Performance Practice, listen back and identify parts that need improvement. Work on those parts during Technical Practice. Then go back to Performance Practice, record it, listen back, work on Technical Practice, rinse and repeat.

Time your performance. You never want to overstay your time slot.

PERFORMING TIPS

To physically prepare for a performance, train like an athlete. Stay fit, drink water, and sleep sufficiently. Singers should exercise and sing at the same time to build stamina. On the day of a performance, eat like an athlete. Four hours before the show, have a balanced meal and plenty of water and then don't have anything else. Promoters may offer meals to musicians before the concert and provide alcohol backstage. Be like a baseball player, not a fan, don't have hot dogs and beer before a game. Everyone else is partying, but you're working.

When memorizing lyrics, imagine the song is a movie. During a show, "watch the movie". This will make for a better performance, because you're not thinking about the audience or anything extraneous to the storytelling.

If you're a singer with no place to warm up your vocals before a show, hum scales and songs. The quiet vibration warms up your voice nearly as well as singing out loud.

In the intro of a song, add a prominent note in the instrumental matching the first note of the vocals. This gives a marker to help you sing the first note in tune. If you're backing a vocalist, do them a favor and cue them on their first note and in places where the singer has difficulty staying in tune. This little trick boosts the confidence and strength of the singer and will make you a go-to sideman.

If you're a lead singer, add a little vocal riff in the intro for an undetectable microphone check. This helps you locate your first note and introduces your vocal tone to the audience.

When performing, intensify emotion by focusing on poignant parts of the storyline. What is your facial expression and body language conveying at important points in the song? Are you physically expressing the emotion you're singing? Is there a gesture or physical movement that does a better job at communicating the message? Practice a facial expression or gesture at key points. Don't be subtle, play to the back of the house, even if it feels like you're exaggerating. This is a basic acting technique, using physicality, not just words. It can reduce or eliminate stage fright, while dramatically increasing the emotional impact on the audience.

When playing an instrument, focus on the feeling in your fingertips. When singing, put your attention on the nearness of your mouth to the microphone. In Spanish, instead of saying "play an instrument", they say "tocar un instrumento", which literally means "touch an instrument". During a performance, experience the sensuous touch of the instrument. This increases intimacy, mesmerizing an audience. It's more alluring than performing in an extroverted way, where attention is on the listener.

When singing onstage, don't move your eyes frequently. Look directly at one single person for a few lines, or a whole verse, and sing only to them. Then look at another person for the next few lines. Even if spotlights are too bright to see an individual face, don't just gaze at people in front of the stage. Look out to the back of the crowd and imagine someone is connecting to you with their eyes. This translates as more intimate than addressing the whole audience at once.

When you make a mistake in a performance, double down and repeat it. A missed note, a wrong chord, an incorrect lyric, don't let these inevitable occurrences throw you off. Never admit self-criticism to an audience, whether you're on- or off-stage. They don't want to know your mistakes; they want to adore you. Stay in the mood and don't let that magic bubble pop.

"Being in the moment" is the power of a live show. As a performer, you are responsible for providing that experience to the audience. The only way to succeed is to practice the song, not until you can play it right, but until you can't play it wrong. Practice gives you the confidence to let go onstage, forget technique and get lost in the moment. If the song transports you, the audience will come along for the ride. For music to really move people, being present is the single most important thing to achieve.

SONGWRITING TIPS

Skilled use of repetition and variation is a hallmark of memorable songwriting. Internal rhymes and alliteration are repetitions that make a song easier to learn.

Use prosody to add depth, finding musical interpretations of lyrics.

Add a lift to give a musical alert that the chorus is approaching.

In an instrumental or vocal riff, echo the melody from the hook or verse. The repetition of melody makes for a catchier song, because it's easier to remember.

Choose words in the realm of the central theme. But be subtle, don't write a laundry list of metaphors. Have a conversation, don't drone on like a thesaurus.

Rhyme the hook to strengthen it.

After writing lyrics, experiment by changing the perspective. If the story is told in first person, try it in third person. If it's about the past, try it in the present. If it's a sad song, try switching it to happy. If it's from a woman's point of voice, try making it so a man sings it.

Build a storyboard by summarizing each section in a single sentence. Read the sentences in order and check that the story is complete.

Who is the singer's character? The person has to be likeable otherwise few artists will want to perform the song and even the listeners will shut down. Who is the singer talking to, not the audience, but inside the story? It's usually best not to preach or recite poetry, only communicate. Why is the singer telling the story? Why is it important they tell the story now? Backstory creates a backdrop.

Check if your title is original or cliché. Type your hook into the ASCAP and BMI title search and you can see how many songs have been registered with that title. A title can't be copyrighted, but I prefer originality.

Brainstorm lyrics that are focused by following threads in a thesaurus, then looking up pertinent words in a rhyming dictionary.

Pay attention to where a sentence begins, on, before or after the downbeat. Each section can have a different beginning point from the other sections to differentiate it. Begin a new section on an alternate chord to announce the change.

Save a note in the melody for the hook, a note that isn't used elsewhere in the song. Save the words in the title for the hook, don't use them elsewhere in the song.

Look for places to put sparkle and "ear candy". Add alliteration, internal rhymes, and prosody. Include "furniture", images conveying the physical world where the story takes place. Include conversational idioms and unusual vocabulary.

Compose melodies that are fun to sing. Use notes well inside a singer's vocal range. Build spaces to breathe into the lyrics.

When rewriting a song, find the best part and repeat it. Repeat a vocal melody as an instrumental.

If songwriting is your true passion, you might experience a shift in time perception while writing or performing. You may feel like time has stopped; an hour can feel like a minute. I think of it as an Einstein-relativity-type phenomenon.

Read lyrics out loud, without singing, to make sure the emphasis of each word is conversational.

After a song is complete, go back through every line to check for dull zones. If something sounds mediocre, rewrite it until every word gives you chills. Compete with yourself to make every line your favorite, no filler. Make the second verse better than the first. Add hooks everywhere, not just in the chorus, by writing clever phrases, catchy melodies, and instrumental riffs.

Add dimensions to make sure a song isn't flat from start to finish. Give it shape by varying emotion, volume, intensity, density, or pitch. When you get to the first chorus, don't over sing it, leave some headroom for the following choruses to be even more powerful. Make each chorus have a different angle, moving the story forward.

Increasing intensity doesn't mean increasing volume. Holding back can make a listener lean in; sudden silence is dramatic. A new chord, a change of key, or a note that hasn't been used yet will grab attention.

The arrangement at the end of a song is often predictable, the singer finishes and then the band ties it up. A song doesn't have to end with a flourish or a fade. To try a different approach, use a technique I call "letting the bottom fall off". When you get to the end of the song, the band abruptly stops playing and "lets the bottom fall off" leaving the singer to finish unaccompanied. This adds "ear candy" to the finale, because it's unexpected.

Find the point of maximum intensity, often near the last chorus. When the moment comes, take it up a notch and make it even more intense. Go from touching to wrenching, from soaring to rocketing. When you've milked the moment as hard as you can, give the singer a "money note". That's what the music industry calls the apex of a song that fans pay to hear. If done correctly, the audience responds noticeably.

I'm an introvert with no stage fright, which I used to think was an anomaly. But as part of a community of songwriters, I've come to realize that most of us are introverted. The desire to express ourselves drives us, as opposed to lead singers who thrive on being the center of attention. The psychology of songwriters is often super-sensitive and emotional. Maybe that's what it takes to be a writer.

Don't seek outside validation, unless you are prepared for the emotional impact. When someone doesn't like your song, or worse yet, doesn't respond in any way, it can hurt a lot. Regardless of how much success you have, somebody is going to dislike you. On the flip side, if you like your own song, somebody will no doubt like it too.

Remember your dreams, songwriting can happen in your sleep.

PARTING THOUGHTS

In Writing Lyrics In A Grid, we discussed aspects of songwriting that aren't taught elsewhere. Because using visual patterns to analyze lyrics is a new concept, this book had to be methodical, like a manual or a textbook.

Some songwriters focus too much on technicality, which can make music dull. Some focus too much on inspiration, which can make a song weak. Find your own balance between raw creativity and meticulous crafting.

I have a satisfying feeling at completing a book that makes a unique contribution to the existing knowledge base of songwriting craft. My highest honor would be seeing Writing Lyrics In A Grid in a well-rounded collection on the subject, on a shelf wedged between books that have taught me so much.

The method of writing lyrics in a grid has been an essential tool. It took a long while to develop the trade secret and even longer to share it with anyone. But I'm not keeping to myself anymore and it feels good to let it out from inside my head.

I sincerely hope this technique has a positive impact on your songwriting. If your writing improves using my method, I'd love to hear from you.

In conclusion, I leave you with the words I tell myself daily:

Keep on writing.

Don't stop writing.

Keep writing.

APPENDIX I
BIOGRAPHY

NOMI YAH is a songwriter and author. She co-wrote King Of Kings, currently with Universal Music Group. The song was recorded by the band Petra on their album Petra Praise: The Rock Cries Out. It earned a gold record, was top ten on the charts for a year, and won a Dove Award. Nomi was a teenager when she wrote that song and signed her first publishing deal with Maranatha Music.

She performed for twenty-five years and played nearly two thousand shows with a wide range of artists from Eek-A-Mouse to The Flying Karamazov Brothers. She toured nationally and internationally. She co-wrote Prison with Eek-A-Mouse on the Eeksperience album. She co-wrote A Man First on the compilation album Made In Amerikkka, featuring Snoop Dogg.

Nomi has been signed or affiliated with such publishers as Maranatha Music, Word, Universal, Capitol, EMI, Brentwood-Benson, Gospel Music Coalition, Corinthian Group, The Copyright Company, CCLI. She won awards including the ASCAP Plus Popular Music Award five times, Tonos A&R Pick, Sherrill C. Corwin Metropolitan Theaters Writing Award, Creative Arts Academic Award. She was an extra in the movie Marilyn: The Untold Story.

Her songs have been on Comcast cable commercials, MTV reality shows, the Sundance channel and independent films, including Champion Bubbla, Jammin For Jamaica, Island Paradise. She has been on radio stations including KPFA, KALX, KMFB, Cabo Mil Radio, KSVY.

She has been a promoter for clubs and festivals, including Ashkenaz in Berkeley and Palookaville in Santa Cruz. For thirteen years, she volunteered with the West Coast

Songwriters, hosting song-screenings at the annual conference and managing the monthly songwriting competition for the Berkeley Chapter at the Freight & Salvage. She co-founded Song Brigade, a song development company.

Nomi Yah has authored several books. Notes To Notes: How I Went From Music To Real Estate, is a memoir, released in 2019. The audiobook, narrated by the author, was released in 2020. The Nomi Yah Songbook is a songbook of original songs, released in 2013. Revolutionary Wanker was an early eighties punk magazine. Living In Shashamane by Anne Marie Hamilton is a memoir of repatriation.

Nomi founded Elohe Homes LLC, a real estate investment company. She lives in Sonoma, California.

SOME ARTISTS NOMI WORKED WITH

Adam Nielson, Adam Traum, Ahkil Mustafa, Ameir Smith, Amlak Tafari, Ana Coates, Andrew Adair Milne, Ann Rosencranz, Area Leader Music Syndicate, Ashling Cole, Azeem, Beth Custer, Blaque Ice, Brimstone, Cameron Stymist, Cannon (Lion of Judah), Caribbean Vibe, Cheb I Sabbah, Chika Shimojima, Chris Strap-On, Claytoven, Clocks, C Major Group, Contraband, Culture Kanute, CSBV, Dan Ashley, Danilo, Dark Circus, Dave Maurichat, Denis Louiseau, Dennis D' Menace, Dr. Jinglez, Dread and the Chosen Few, Eek-A-Mouse, Elio Schiavo, Emsley Fraser (Razor Blade), Eva Snyder, Faisel, Found Objects, Foundation, Genie Majeeda, George and the Wonders, Glorianna Opera Company, Grand Son Demus, Gulf Of The Farralones, Hookstown Brown, Hurricane Gilbert, Invertebrates, Itals, Jacob's Descendents, James Gardiner, Jeff Cuda, Jeff "4-way" Miller (Bad Posture), Jeff Mooney, Jess Curtis, John Mazzei, Josh Friedman, Jules Beckman (Blue Man Group), Junior B, Keith Hennessy, Karamazov Brothers (Fighting Instruments Of Karma), Ken Switalski, Kristyle, Kulture Kanute, Kwama Roots Mama, Lady Saw, Lennon Leppert, Lennox Brown (Buppy and the Uplifters), Lickshot, Lionel Randolph, Lisa Abraham, Lisa

Mischke, Living Theater, Locura De Amor, Love Goat, Lucky Kat, Majah P, Majestic, Major Terror, Malaika Wanag, Marcus Barone, Maria Kirizian, Mark Eitzel (American Music Club), Melbourne, Mike Lounibos, Moon Has Fat Thighs, Nao Bustamante, Nina Wise, Obeyjah, Oonka Symeon, Phil Nudelman, Quinn Martin, Ralph Eno (The Twitchers), Ralph Kinsey (Kinsey Report), Rachel Kaplan, Rankin Joe, Ras D, Raskidus, Ras Midas, Red I, Richard Marriott (Club Foot Orchestra), Ron Brown (Hookstown Brown), Rusty Water Dream Band, Ryan Daisley, Sarah Shelton Mann, Sharon Matthews, Sister I Live, Sly Fox, Sonar Eclipse, Song Brigade, Sophie Conty, Stanya Kahn, Starhawk (Black Cat Band), Stevie Love, Sweet Chocolate, Tequila, The Backups, Theater of Changes, Theater Action Group (TAG), Thousand Days Of Shame, Tribal Warning, Toho, Tony D, Traumschuhe, Trinity Rayne, Triplex, Twelve Year Olds, Twisted Roots, Unda P, Vince Black, Wadi Gad, Wil Key, XSample, YahWanag, Yellow Wall Dub, Zoe and Molly Flores (Starflightrocks).

SOME ARTISTS NOMI SHARED THE BILL WITH

Abyssinians, Alpha Blondy, Andrew Tosh, Anthony B, Arkansas Man, Barry Valentino, Bedlam Rovers, Ben Bacot, Born Jamericans, Buju Banton, Chris Isaak, Clan Dyken, Dominique Baraka, Donny Rasta (Roots Vibration), Elbows Akimbo, Frankie Paul, Fully Fullwood Band, Grandson Demus, Higher Heights, Invertebrates, Israel Vibrations, Itals, J. Scott, Jah Levi, Junior Toots, King Caleb, Kingston 12, Kosono, KuKuKu, Leon Caldero, Lucky Dube, Luciano, Makka B, Mad Professor, Michael Franti, Michael Rose, Mighty Diamonds, Mimimal Man, Pato Banton, Rankin Scroo and Ginger, Reggae Angels, Sanchez, Scropes, Sean Paul, Skatalites, Sly and Robbie, Stacy Golden, Steve Seskin, Taco Wagon, The Dave, Trini-Kid, Vibes Supreme, Wailers, Yami Bolo, Zodiac Sound.

SOME VENUES WHERE NOMI PERFORMED

CALIFORNIA

<u>Alameda</u> - Island Paradise

<u>Belmont</u> - Chris' New Harbor

<u>Berkeley</u> - Ashkenaz, Club Chibbo, Freight & Salvage, Juneteenth Festival, Seen Festival at People's Park, University of California Berkeley

<u>Boulder Creek</u> - Boulder Creek Brewery

<u>Chico</u> - Chico State University

<u>Concord</u> – Brian Wilson Vigil

<u>Davis</u> - University of California Davis

<u>Fresno</u> – Club Fred

<u>Isla Vista</u>- Borsodi's

<u>La Honda</u> – Greenpeace Benefit

<u>Los Angeles</u> – Key Club, Kulak's Woodshed, Roxy Theater, The Gig, Universal Studio City

<u>Mendocino</u> – Greenwood Theater Company, Glorianna Opera Company, Helen Schoeni Theater at the Mendocino Art Center, Mendocino High School, Preston Hall

<u>Monterey</u> - Monterey Bay Reggae Festival

<u>Mount Shasta</u> – Mount Shasta World Music Festival

<u>Oakland</u> - Club Jjang Ga, Continental Club, FM Smith Recreation Center, Reggae in the Hills, Sweet Jimmy's, Uptown Nightclub

<u>Palo Alto</u> - Fanny & Alexander's

<u>Pamona</u> – Glass House

<u>Petaluma</u> – Pheonix Theater

<u>Sacramento</u> - Jamaica House, Red Lion Inn, Ricki's, Scratch 8, Annual Harvest Festival, Ocean Lounge, Stoney Inn, Club Element, OK Universe Sports Complex, Cheers Lounge, RoadHouse

<u>San Diego</u> - Belly Up Tavern, House Of Blues, Viejas Casino, Wave House

<u>Santa Ana</u> - Galaxy

<u>San Francisco</u> – 509 Club, Bamboo Hut, Blue House, Club Foot, Compound, Eagles Tavern, El Rio, Fort Mason, Great American Music Hall, Haight Street Fair, Jelly's, Jillian's At The Metreon, Juneteenth Festival on Fillmore, Klub Komotion, Mabuhay Gardens, Maritime Hall, New College, On Broadway, Paradise

Lounge, Pier 23, Rad Cult Fest, Reggae in Golden Gate Park, Shotwell Rogue Loft, Slim's, Sound of Music, Storyville, Valencia Tool and Die, San Francisco Women's Building, Suburban Palace, The Blue House, Full Moon Saloon, Pier 50, New College, I-Hotel, ATA Gallery, Julian Theater, Studio #4, 509 Cultural Center

San Jose – Waves, Agenda Lounge, Club Ibex, Fuel, Cesar Chavez Plaza

San Juan Capistrano - The Coach House

San Leandro - Kicks

San Rafael – Fourth Street Tavern

Santa Barbara - The Coach House, The Shack

Santa Cruz - University of California Santa Cruz, Positively Front Street, Vet's Hall, Catalyst, Palookaville, Brookdale Lodge, San Lorenzo Park, AIDS Walk, Greenpeace Music Festival, Santa Cruz Farmer's Market, Louden Nelson Center, Pacific Cultural Center

Santa Rosa – Sonoma County Fair

Sonoma – The Moose, Sonoma Springs Brewery, Hanna's Boys Center, Kivelstadt Cellars

COLORADO
Boulder - Tulagi

ENGLAND
Canterbury
London

GERMANY
Berlin – Theaterfestival Berliner in Ballhaus Tiergarten, Hochschule de Kunst, Neue HDK

HOLLAND
Amsterdam

MARYLAND
Baltimore - 8X10 Room

MASSACHUSETTES
Cambridge - House of Blues
Nantucket - The Muse
Northampton - Pearl Street
Oaks Bluff – The Lamp Post

MEXICO
Cabo San Lucas – Cabo Wabo, Cabo Mil Festival

MICHIGAN
Royal Oak - Fifth Avenue Billiards

NEW YORK
New York City - Joe's Pub at the Public Theater, Brooklyn Believer's Church, Brooklyn College
Buffalo – Calumet

NORTH CAROLINA
Kill Devil Hills - Port-O-Call
Wilmington - Saxons By The River

OHIO
Cleveland - Agora Theater

OREGON
Eugene – The Wild Duck, Oregon Country Fair, Wow Hall
Portland – Berbati's Pan, Roseland Theater
RHODE ISLAND
Matunuck - Ocean Mist

SOUTH CAROLINA
Charleston - The Music Farm

SPAIN
Cadeques – Los Pirates, La Belle Epoche
Barcelona
Empuriabrava – Malibu Club
Gerona

<u>Rosas</u>

TENNESSEE
<u>Nashville</u> - Nashville Songwriter's Festival on Music Row, Curb Records, American Songwriter Magazine, Sure Fire Music

UTAH
<u>Salt Lake City</u> - Safari Club

VIRGINIA
<u>Hampton</u> - Mill Point Park

WASHINGTON
<u>Seattle</u> – Bohemian Club, Doc Maynards

APPENDIX 2
GLOSSARY

<u>Alliteration</u> - The occurrence of the same letter or sound at the beginning of adjacent or closely connected words.

<u>Artist</u> - A person who practices any of the creative arts. In music, the "artist" often refers to the lead singer.

<u>Bar</u> - A single unit of time containing a specific number of beats. For example, a bar may have four beats.

<u>Beat</u> - A rhythmic stress in music. Also, a song's underlying instrumental track.

<u>Bridge</u> - A musical passage linking two sections of a composition.

<u>Chorus</u> - The main part of a popular song that is repeated after each verse, typically containing a song's signature musical motif and primary lyrical message.

<u>Double-Time</u> - A rhythmic feel that makes songs sound twice as fast by doubling the amount of beats.

<u>Downbeat</u> - An accented beat, usually the first of the bar.

<u>External Rhyme</u> - A rhyme involving words at the end of lines.

<u>Genre</u> - A category of artistic composition, as in music or literature, characterized by similarities in form, style or content.

<u>Headroom</u> - The amount of space in dB that a mixing engineer leaves for a mastering engineer to properly process and alter an audio signal.

Homonym - Each of two or more words having the same pronunciation but different meanings.

Hook - A short lyrical line or melodic phrase used to make a song memorable and catch the attention of the listener. The title of a song is often the hook.

Improvise – An immediate musical composition, which combines performance with communication of emotions and instrumental technique as well as spontaneous response to other musicians.

In The Pocket - Being in the groove, at the right tempo and volume. The point at which every element of a song comes together and feels just right.

Internal Rhyme - A rhyme involving words in the middle of lines.

Intro - A passage that opens a song, preceding the lyrics.

Lift - A song section with a musical rise in pitch and emotion, often a pre-chorus.

Phrasing - The act, method, or result of grouping notes into musical phrases to allow expression. The rhythmic placement of syllables in lyrics.

Pick-Up - One or more syllables at the beginning of a line of lyrics that are regarded as preliminary to, and not a part of, the metrical pattern. In musical terminology, a pick-up is an "anacrusis".

Pre-Chorus - A short section between a verse and a chorus, with the main purpose of building energy, often the lift.

Prosody – The composition of melody that reflects lyrical content. For example, when the lyrics say the word "up", the melody goes up.

Publisher - A person in the business or profession of the commercial production and issuance of literature, information, musical scores or recordings, or art.

Riff – A short instrumental melody.

Scratch – A recording of an instrumental or vocal track that will be replaced.

Sideman - A supporting musician in a band.

Song - A short musical composition of words and music.

Songwriter - A person who writes lyrics and/or music for songs.

Syllabalizing - A process of using visual patterns to write lyrics. Patterns are formed by writing syllables of lyrics in a grid. The author coined this word.

Syncopated - A displacement of the regular metrical accent in music, caused typically by stressing the weak beat.

Synonym - A word or phrase that means exactly, or nearly the same, as another word or phrase.

Tag - A dramatic variation in the last section of the song. A tag is analogical to a "coda" in classical music.

Topline - The vocal melody and lyrics of a song. A topliner, or topline songwriter, provides a melody and lyric for a producer's instrumental track.

Track - A recorded song. Or a song's underlying instrumental music. Or a single instrument in a recording.

Triangulating - The use of three songs to create a template for a new song. The author coined this meaning.

<u>Verse</u> - A verse is a repeated section of a song that typically features a new set of lyrics on each repetition. The music of a verse is often written to complement the chorus music.

<u>Vertical</u> - A part of a song's composition that rises in pitch and soars to an emotional climax, often in a chorus.

APPENDIX 3
LYRICS

Throughout this book, we worked with original songs and those in the public domain. Often, we didn't discuss the entire song, so here are the full lyrics of those songs.

ANGELS WE HAVE HEARD ON HIGH
James Chadwick (Chapter 4)

Angels we have heard on high
Sweetly singing o'er the plains
And the mountains in reply
Echoing their joyous strains

    Gloria, in excelsis Deo
    Gloria, in excelsis Deo

Shepherds, why this jubilee?
Why your joyous strain prolongs?
What the gladsome tidings be
Which inspire your heavenly songs?

    Gloria, in excelsis Deo
    Gloria, in excelsis Deo

Come to Bethlehem and see
Him whose birth the angels sing
Come adore on bended knee
Christ the Lord, the newborn king

    Gloria, in excelsis Deo
    Gloria, in excelsis Deo

BOBBY SHAFTO

Traditional (Chapter 4)

Bobby Shafto's gone to sea
Silver buckles at his knee
He'll come back and marry me
Pretty Bobby Shafto

Bobby Shafto's bright and fair
Combing down his yellow hair
He's my love for evermore
Pretty Bobby Shafto

Bobby Shafto's tall and slim
He's always dressed so neat and trim
The ladies they all kick at him
Pretty Bobby Shafto

Bobby Shafto's gettin' a bairn
For to dangle on his arm
In his arm and on his knee
Bobby Shafto loves me

COULDN'T WALK AWAY

Nomi Yah (Chapter 10)

I don't believe I was naïve
When I believed our love was true
But life is like a library
You're always learning something new
You did me wrong, I would be gone
Considering what you put me through
I made a choice and right or wrong
Depends upon your point of view

> I couldn't walk, walk away from you
> Couldn't walk away, couldn't walk away
> I couldn't walk, walk away from you

Couldn't walk away, couldn't walk away

I had to think about day in, day out
The times they really flew
As sweet as notes I blow in holes I made
In flutes made of bamboo
'Though friends of mine are asking
Why I am not using my I.Q.
How can they guess the way I'm blessed
To be a part of me and you

      I couldn't walk, walk away from you
      Couldn't walk away, couldn't walk away
      I couldn't walk, walk away from you
      Couldn't walk away, couldn't walk away

I had to stay, I could see no other way
To be happy in a big wide lonely land
A man with no woman, a woman with no man
Love is happiness and my obsession
Lack or loss thereof will cause depression

      I couldn't walk, walk away from you
      Couldn't walk away, couldn't walk away
      I couldn't walk, walk away from you
      Couldn't walk away, couldn't walk away

HAPPY BIRTHDAY
Patty Hill, Mildred J. Hill (Chapter 14)

Happy birthday to you
Happy birthday to you
Happy birthday, happy birthday
Happy birthday to you

MARY HAD A LITTLE LAMB
Lowell Mason (Chapter 4)

Mary had a little lamb
Little lamb, little lamb
Mary had a little lamb
Its fleece was white as snow
And everywhere that Mary went
Mary went, Mary went
Everywhere that Mary went
The lamb was sure to go

He followed her to school one day
School one day, school one day
He followed her to school one day
Which was against the rules
It made the children laugh and play
Laugh and play, laugh and play
It made the children laugh and play
To see a lamb at school

And so, the teacher turned it out
Turned it out, turned it out
And so, the teacher turned it out
But still it lingered near
He waited patiently about
Patiently about, patiently about
He waited patiently about
'Til Mary did appear

And then he ran to her and laid
Her and laid, her and laid
And then he ran to her and laid
His head upon her arm
As if he said "I'm not afraid
Not afraid, not afraid"
As if he said "I'm not afraid
You'll keep me from all harm"

"What makes the lamb love Mary so?
Mary so? Mary so?
What makes the lamb love Mary so?"
The eager children cried
"Why, Mary loves the lamb you know
Lamb you know, lamb you know
Why, Mary loves the lamb, you know"
The teacher did reply

MY COUNTRY 'TIS OF THEE
Samuel Francis Smith (Chapter 14)

My country 'tis of thee
Sweet land of liberty, of thee I sing
Land where my fathers died
Land of the pilgrims' pride
From every mountainside, let freedom ring

My native country thee
Land of the noble free, thy name I love
I love thy rocks and rills
Thy woods and templed hills
My heart with rapture thrills, like that above

Let music swell the breeze
And ring from all the trees, sweet freedom's song
Let mortal tongues awake
Let all that breathe partake
Let rocks their silence break, the sound prolong

Our fathers' God to Thee
Author of liberty, to Thee we sing
Long may our land be bright
With freedom's holy light
Protect us by Thy might, great God our King

Our joyful hearts today

Their grateful tribute pay, happy and free
After our toils and fears
After our blood and tears
Strong with our hundred years, oh God, to Thee

OLD MACDONALD
Thomas D'Urley (Chapter 4)

Old MacDonald had a farm, E-I-E-I-O
And on his farm, he had a cow, E-I-E-I-O
With a moo moo here and a moo moo there
Here a moo, there a moo, everywhere a moo moo
Old MacDonald had a farm, E-I-E-I-O

Old MacDonald had a farm, E-I-E-I-O
And on his farm, he had a pig, E-I-E-I-O
With an oink oink here and an oink oink there
Here an oink, there an oink, everywhere an oink oink
Old MacDonald had a farm, E-I-E-I-O

Old MacDonald had a farm, E-I-E-I-O
And on his farm, he had a duck, E-I-E-I-O
With a quack quack here and a quack quack there
Here a quack, there a quack, everywhere a quack quack
Old MacDonald had a farm, E-I-E-I-O

Old MacDonald had a farm, E-I-E-I-O
And on his farm, he had a horse, E-I-E-I-O
With a neigh neigh here and a neigh neigh there
Here a neigh, there a neigh, everywhere a neigh neigh
Old MacDonald had a farm, E-I-E-I-O

Old MacDonald had a farm, E-I-E-I-O
And on his farm, he had a lamb, E-I-E-I-O
With a baa baa here and a baa baa there
Here a baa, there a baa, everywhere a baa baa
Old MacDonald had a farm, E-I-E-I-O

Old MacDonald had a farm, E-I-E-I-O
And on his farm, he had some chickens, E-I-E-I-O
With a cluck cluck here and a cluck cluck there
Here a cluck, there a cluck, everywhere a cluck cluck
Old MacDonald had a farm, E-I-E-I-O

Old MacDonald had a farm, E-I-E-I-O
And on his farm, he had some dogs, E-I-E-I-O
With a bow wow here and a bow wow there
Here a bow, there a wow, everywhere a bow wow
Cluck cluck here and a cluck cluck there
Here a cluck, there a cluck, everywhere a cluck cluck
Baa baa here and a baa baa there
Here a baa, there a baa, everywhere a baa baa
Neigh neigh here and a neigh neigh there
Here a neigh, there a neigh, everywhere a neigh neigh
Quack quack here and a quack quack there
Here a quack, there a quack, everywhere a quack quack
Oink oink here and an oink oink there
Here an oink, there an oink, everywhere an oink oink
Moo moo here and a moo moo there
Here a moo, there a moo, everywhere a moo moo
Old MacDonald had a farm, E-I-E-I-O

PERFECT ENOUGH
Nomi Yah (Chapters 6, 7, 8 and 9)

Your child gets tall, while you are busy
Think of it, isn't it really a shame
If you're missing it all, childhood is brief
Picture books and loose teeth
And that Little League game, man relax

    Life is perfect enough
    Perfect enough, Lord
    It could be better, sometimes it's rough
    But today is perfect enough

Your Jaguar's fast but you're running late
You won't catch the plane but you'll get on the next
And you'll fly first-class, trying to achieve
The American Dream
While you're piling up debts, man relax

Life is perfect enough
Perfect enough, Lord
It could be better, sometimes it's rough
But today is perfect enough

You should be proud of what you've done
Look how far you've come
It's all a matter of priority, keep up what you're doing
If it doesn't ruin the time that you spend
With your family, you are their rock
And they love when you walk
Through that door at the end of the day

Life is perfect enough
Perfect enough, Lord
It could be better, sometimes it's rough
But today is perfect enough

ROCK-A-BYE BABY
Mother Goose (Chapter 14)

Rock-a-bye baby in the tree top
When the wind blows, the cradle will rock
When the bough breaks, the cradle will fall
And down will come baby, cradle and all

ROW ROW ROW
Eliphalet Oram Lyte (Chapter 14)

Row, row, row your boat, gently down the stream
Merrily, merrily, merrily, merrily, life is but a dream

ROWS OF ROSES
Nomi Yah (Chapter 5)

When grandpa proposed, he gave her a rose
On their wedding day, he gave a big bouquet
On anniversaries, he went to nurseries
Every year he chose a different color rose
To put in the ground for her
For fifty years

    She has rows of roses growing in her garden
    She has rows of roses planted in her yard
    She cuts and puts them in a vase
    It puts a smile on her face
    To see those rows and rows of roses

As grandpa would say, a store-bought bouquet
Doesn't last for long, now even though he's gone
He still gives flowers to her
For the rest of her years

    She has rows of roses growing in her garden
    She has rows of roses planted in her yard
    She cuts and puts them in a vase
    It puts a smile on her face
    To see those rows and rows of roses

We said come live with us, she wouldn't budge
She decided to stay where she was
Where she could breathe his undying love, his undying love

    She has rows of roses growing in her garden
    She has rows of roses planted in her yard
    She cuts and puts them in a vase
    It puts a smile on her face
    To see those rows and rows of roses

<u>SLIDE</u>
Nomi Yah (Chapter 13)

Told you once, I told you twice
I don't get off on games and lies
'Though you tried, you couldn't hide
I can't let it slide, can't let it slide

I wasn't looking for trouble
I was out going shopping in the mall
Buying something to surprise you
But I was surprised at what I saw
You were pushing up on a man I didn't even know
Two-faced on double duty
Not the woman I'd have sworn I know
I must have been tricked by your beauty

Told you once, I told you twice
I don't get off on games and lies
'Though you tried, you couldn't hide
I can't let it slide, can't let it slide

Just this morning I asked you
To go out tonight on a date
Told you to get dressed special
But I got slapped by the hand of fate
So, I had to cancel the reservations
The same place my own father proposed
Had to go back and return the diamonds
I had to toss out a dozen roses

Told you once, I told you twice
I don't get off on games and lies
'Though you tried, you couldn't hide
I can't let it slide, can't let it slide

TAKE A DAY OFF
Nomi Yah (Chapter 11)

All that stuff you have to do now
Can't it wait until tomorrow
All we ever do is work
Don't you think that we deserve
An occasional time out
We're going to be playing hooky, calling in sick
Doing whatever we need to be together

>Take a day, take a day, take a day off
>It's time for getting in the sun
>It's time for getting nothing done
>Take a day, take a day, take a day off
>We're going to finally get a break
>We're going to finally get to take a day off

Putting E&J in Pepsi
Kicking it and getting tipsy
We'll be acting juvenile
Like it's going out of style
I just love when you're with me
We're going to be playing hooky, calling in sick
Doing whatever we need to be together

>Take a day, take a day, take a day off
>It's time for getting in the sun
>It's time for getting nothing done
>Take a day, take a day, take a day off
>We're going to finally get a break
>We're going to finally get to take a day off

I don't mean to make you delinquent
But I want to say what I'm thinking

>Take a day, take a day, take a day off
>It's time for getting in the sun
>It's time for getting nothing done

Take a day, take a day, take a day off
We're going to finally get a break
We're going to finally get to take a day off

TWINKLE TWINKLE
Jane Taylor (Chapter 12)

Twinkle, twinkle, little star
How I wonder what you are
Up above the world so high
Like a diamond in the sky
Twinkle, twinkle, little star
How I wonder what you are

When the blazing sun is gone
When he nothing shines upon
Then you show your little light
Twinkle, twinkle, all the night
Twinkle, twinkle, little star
How I wonder what you are

Then the traveler in the dark
Thanks you for your tiny spark
He could not see which way to go
If you did not twinkle so
Twinkle, twinkle, little star
How I wonder what you are

In the dark blue sky you keep
Often through my curtains peep
For you never shut your eye
'Til the sun is in the sky
Twinkle, twinkle, little star
How I wonder what you are

As your bright and tiny spark
Lights the traveler in the dark
'Though I know not what you are

Twinkle, twinkle, little star
Twinkle, twinkle, little star
How I wonder what you are

<u>WORTH IT</u>
Nomi Yah (Chapter 1)

I don't want to tell you doubts I have in me
I don't want to bring them to actuality
Maybe I just don't want to lose you
But working it out isn't easy

    It's going to be worth it
    Living in a better time than now
    It's going to be worth it
    Doing the best that we know how
    It's going to be worth it working it out
    It's going to be worth it working it out

When we fight each other, baby, when we disagree
When nobody's listening and nobody can see
No matter how long you've known somebody
You never know them completely

    It's going to be worth it
    Living in a better time than now
    It's going to be worth it
    Doing the best that we know how
    It's going to be worth it working it out
    It's going to be worth it working it out

Running away
Would be easier than learning to stay
Could I live with myself every day
Wipe the slate clean
Forget what you mean, forget what you've been
Forget what we've seen, forget what we dreamed
Ah, but I have a feeling that

It's going to be worth it
Living in a better time than now
It's going to be worth it
Doing the best that we know how
It's going to be worth it working it out
It's going to be worth it working it out

YANKEE DOODLE
George M. Cohan (Chapter 4)

Yankee Doodle went to town a'riding on a pony
Stuck a feather in his cap and called it macaroni

Yankee Doodle, keep it up, Yankee Doodle Dandy
Mind the music and the step and with the girls be handy

Father and I went down to camp, along with Captain Gooding
There were all the men and boys, as thick as hasty pudding

Yankee Doodle, keep it up, Yankee Doodle Dandy
Mind the music and the step and with the girls be handy

And there was Captain Washington upon a strapping stallion
Giving orders to his men, I guess there were a million

Yankee Doodle, keep it up, Yankee Doodle Dandy
Mind the music and the step and with the girls be handy

Yankee Doodle is a tune that comes in mighty handy
The enemy all runs away at Yankee Doodle Dandy

Yankee Doodle, keep it up, Yankee Doodle Dandy
Mind the music and the step and with the girls be handy

APPENDIX 4
GRID EXAMPLES

In this book, some of the songs we analyzed included Rows Of Roses (Chapter 5), Take A Day Off (Chapter 11), and Slide (Chapter 13). The following grids are from my writing sessions for those songs.

Does n't last for ~ long ~~
ev - end — it's g — got the

he still ~ gives —
flow — — — wers — — TO
hen — — — — — fon the
Rest — — — of — — hen
yeas — —

to put — in the
grand — — — on — — —
hen — — — this went on after
fif — — — ty —
yeons

1	2	3	4	5	6	7	8
~~When~~ ~~grand~~	~~pa~~	~~pro~~	~~posed~~				He
~~gove~~	~~A~~	~~red~~	~~r~~				
grand-pa	pa	PR-posed	—	—			When He
gove	A	red	rose				
each	year	he	baght	—	—		Than A
Bush	in	A	pot				
exch	year	he	bought	—	—		Than Another
polon	in	A	pot				
(Grand	pa	would	say	—	—		As A
pro-bught	bou-quet			—	—		

+ — All That Shit you have to
Do — Now — — — —
— — Cant It wont un Til To
No — row — — — —
We could go and walk The streets —
steal The time that rich men seek —
— — We can blow it on nice
wa — ther — — — —
— — peo ple's lives are very y
Dif . ferent — — — —
— — Then we come to the same
end — ing — — — —

Ev ery per son on ly has —
Jus so ma-ny chances at —

Hold Bass Blow it On the nice —
Deck King pop si e and)
Get fine kid sy we will take —
ourand deck ake d cou ple of
Syed iels

Play - hoo ky CALL IN sick -
Do what it takes

Play - hoo ky coll in sick
Do - what EVER IT TAKES - I really wanns
Spend - to day ~ to get -
           ther - - -

PLAY - hoo ky call IN sick -what
E VER IT TAKES - I really wanns
Spend - to day day - to get
get - ther - - take A DAY

PLAYING HOOKY 6
PLAY ING HOO KY call ing IN SICK
- - DO WHAT E VER IT TAKES
- I WANT TO spend TO DAY - TO
ge - THER - -

					TAKE	A	DAY
-	TAKE	A	DAY	-	TAKE	A	-
DAY	-	OFF	-	-	Let's	TAKE	A
DAY	OFF	-	It's	time	For	get -	ting
IN	the	SUN	it's	time	for	get -	ting
Not	thing	done	-	-	Let's	TAKE	A
DAY	OFF	-/	Dis	time	For	mak-	ing
Time	FORBe	- ing	HAP -	PY	and d's	- A	WRAP
					TAKE	A	-
-	-	-	-	-			
DAY	-	OFF	-	-			
			Dis	time	THAT	we	start
no	king	some	free	time	FOR	- g	- ing
HAp	py	and	-	-	take	A	-
DAY	off						

It's time for get-ting in the sun
It's time for get-ting not hing done

It's time for Be-ing Hum an and
For mak ing E-nough Room in life
For tak ing A Day off
To take A

It's time FOR Be-ing Hu-man AND
It's time FOR Mak ing Room in life

ING   MAK
A   TAKE

we de-serve it we should make A
point of mak ing time to take A

we earn a break and we should make
A point of mak-ing time to take

we des erve a break to make a
point of mak-ing time to take a

I	-	WAS	1T	look	ing	-	foR
Lost	-	THis	-	morn	ing	-	I
tro	-	ble	-	-	-	I	wount
Askd	-	you	-	-	-	let's	go
out	-	-	-	shop	ping	in	the
out	-	-	to	night	-	on	A
now	-	-	-	-	-	-	-
date	-	-	-	-	-	-	-
I	-	bought	-	some	thing	to	sur
told	-	you	-	to dress	up	-	-
pose	-	you	-	But	I	was	sur
spe	-	don	-	-	But	I	got
rise	-	-	AT	what	I	-	saw
slipd	-	by	me	hand	d	-	fore

was | — | n't | — | look king | — | for
trou | — | ble | — | — | — |
~~Boy~~ | | | — | | |
Bought | — | some | — | Thing to | — | sur
Rose | — | you | | morning | . | I
Just | — | this | — | | |
asked | — | you | . | get dressed | . | up
told | — | you | — | | |
spec | — | in | — | you to | — | get
I | — | told | — | | |
dressed | — | up | — | to get | — | all
Told | — | you up | | | |
dressed | — | you | — | dress up | — | a
Told | — | the | — | dress shirt | — |
we're | — | that | — | | |
got | — | you | | up and | — | look
Get | — | dressed | — | | |
club | . | so | | up some | — | Thing
Get | — | dressed | — | | |
spec | . | in | — | in some | — | This
dress | — | up | | | |
spec | . | in | | | |

I - was nt look ing - For
trou ble - -
I - bought some thing to - sur
prise - you
list - This

I - was n't look ing - For
tro - ble - -
I - bought - some thing to sur
prise - you
list - This - mom thing - I
asked - you
Told - you to dress up - -
spec - ial

Was - n't - look ing - For
trou - ble - -
I - bought - some thing to sur
prise - you
list - this - mom thing - I
asked - you
Told - you -

I	-	WAS	nt	look	ing	-	foR
Last	-	This	-	Mom	nus	-	I
tro	-	be	-	-	-	I	wont
Asked	-	you	-	-	-	let's	go
out	-	-	-	shop	pny	in	Me
out	-	-	to	night	-	on	A
rusu	-	.	.	-	-	-	-
dore	-	-	-	-	-	-	-
I	-	bought	.	Some	nus	to	sur
todd	-	you	to	dress	up	-	-
prse	-	you	-	But	I	was	sur
spe	-	clor	-	-	But	I	got
prse	-	-	AT	wnt	I	-	saw
slopts	-	by	Me	hand	1	-	fsre

APPENDIX 5
SONGBOOK GRAPHICS

The first time I leaked my secret of writing lyrics in a grid was while writing a songbook. In between the music manuscripts, I added graphics that had grids in the background. That turned out to be way too subtle and nobody even asked about the graphics, which led to the writing of this book. The following are the graphics from the songbook, including art drawn by my young son.

CD INCLUDED
Nomi Yah
SONGBOOK
BENEFITS
COULDN'T WALK AWAY
I'M INSPIRED
IF YOU'RE ALIVE

NOMI YAH Grб B Nomi
NOMI YAH MUSIC

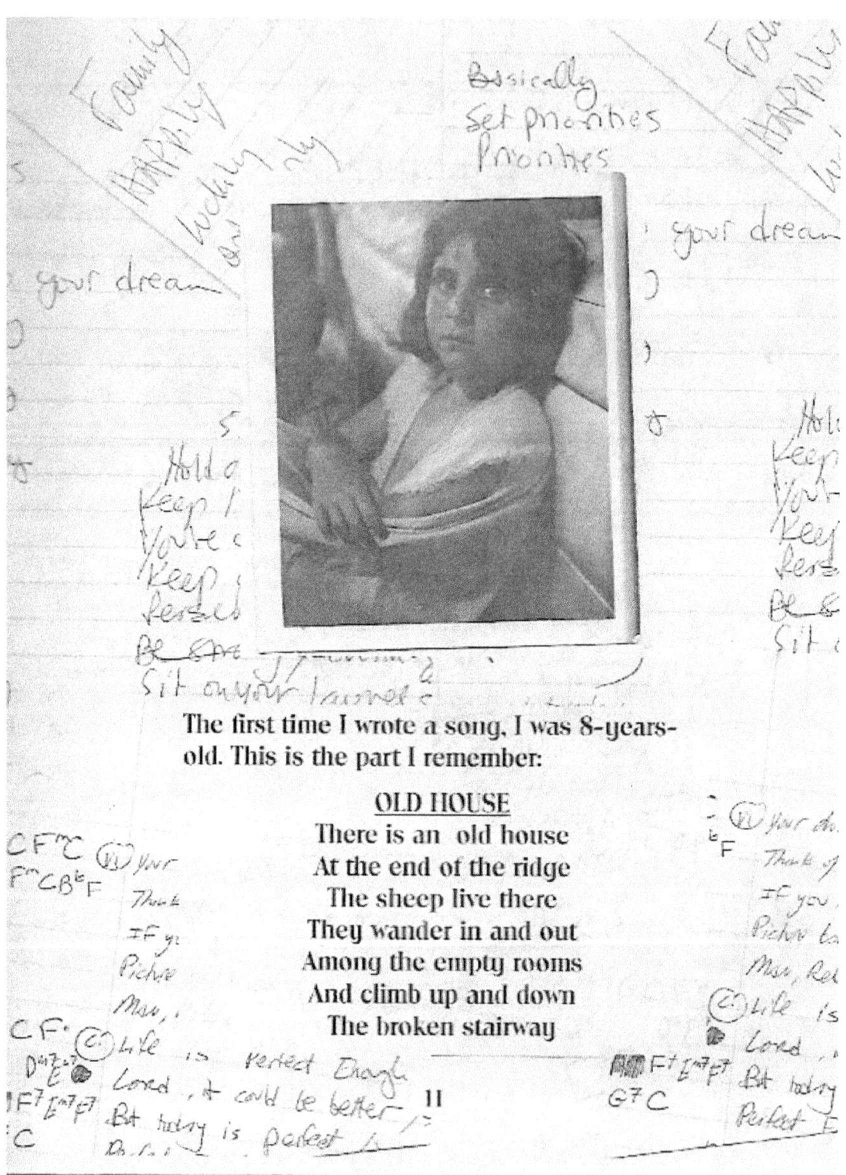

The first time I wrote a song, I was 8-years-old. This is the part I remember:

OLD HOUSE

There is an old house
At the end of the ridge
The sheep live there
They wander in and out
Among the empty rooms
And climb up and down
The broken stairway

318

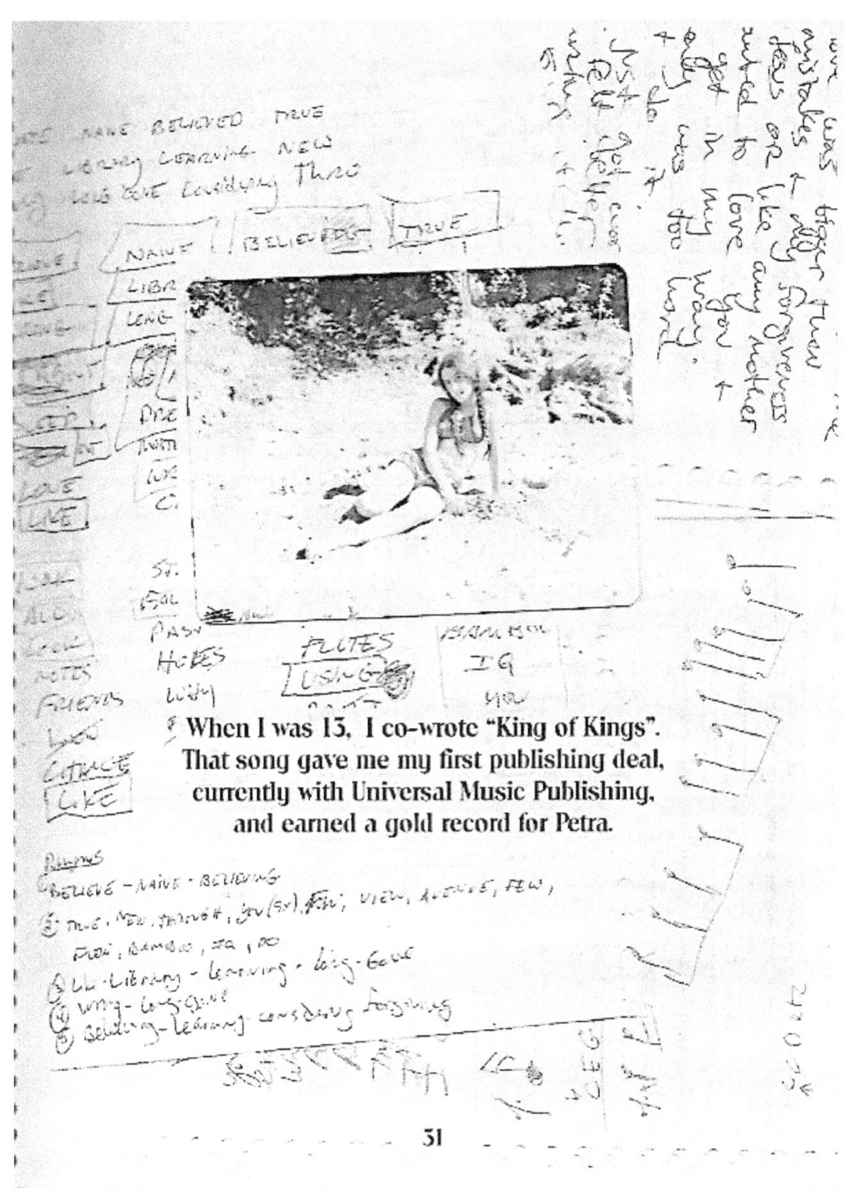

When I was 13, I co-wrote "King of Kings". That song gave me my first publishing deal, currently with Universal Music Publishing, and earned a gold record for Petra.

319

Eek-A-Mouse and I co-wrote the song "Prison" on a tour bus between Salt Lake City and Reno. The song is on the "Eeksperience" album.

I performed at a songwriter festival on Music Row. The stage was on the back porch of Curb Records.

41

Besides performing, I was a concert promoter and worked with many festivals and clubs, including Ashkenaz in Berkeley, Palookaville in Santa Cruz, and Club Foot in San Francisco. This is one of my posters from the 80's.

322

Watching TV on 9/11 I heard a reporter say "Seems like a movie, but it's real." I wrote a song with those words as the chorus and performed it for over 60,000 people in a stadium in Mexico. Thousands sang along, a beautiful sound I'll never forget.

74

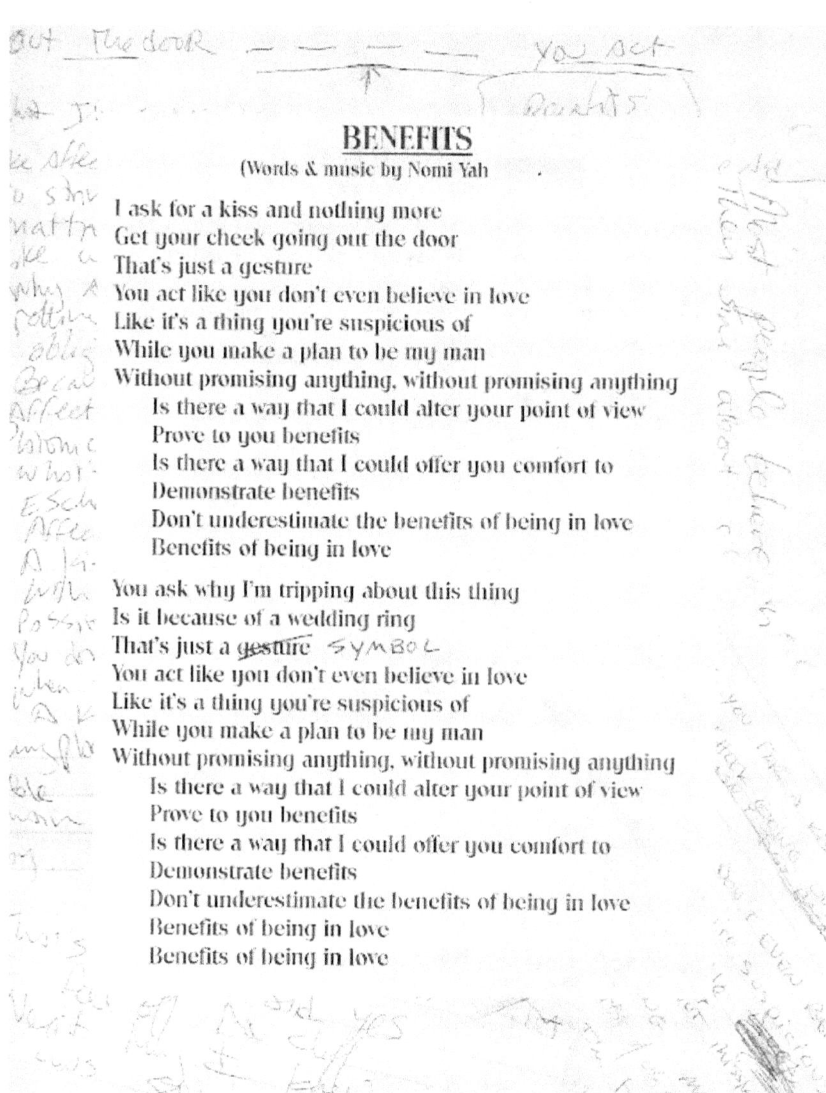

BENEFITS

(Words & music by Nomi Yah)

I ask for a kiss and nothing more
Get your cheek going out the door
That's just a gesture
You act like you don't even believe in love
Like it's a thing you're suspicious of
While you make a plan to be my man
Without promising anything, without promising anything
    Is there a way that I could alter your point of view
    Prove to you benefits
    Is there a way that I could offer you comfort to
    Demonstrate benefits
    Don't underestimate the benefits of being in love
    Benefits of being in love

You ask why I'm tripping about this thing
Is it because of a wedding ring
That's just a gesture
You act like you don't even believe in love
Like it's a thing you're suspicious of
While you make a plan to be my man
Without promising anything, without promising anything
    Is there a way that I could alter your point of view
    Prove to you benefits
    Is there a way that I could offer you comfort to
    Demonstrate benefits
    Don't underestimate the benefits of being in love
    Benefits of being in love
    Benefits of being in love

77

325

COULDN'T WALK AWAY

(Words & music by Nomi Yah)

I don't believe I was naïve when I believed our love was true
But life is like a library, you're always learning something new
You did me wrong, I would be gone, considering what you put me through
I made a choice, and right or wrong depends upon your point of view
    I couldn't walk, walk away from you
    Couldn't walk away, couldn't walk away
    I couldn't walk, walk away from you
    Couldn't walk away, couldn't walk away
    Couldn't walk away, couldn't walk away

I had to think about day in, day out, the times they really flew
As sweet as notes I blow in holes I made in flutes made of bamboo
Though friends of mine are asking why I am not using my IQ
How can they guess the way I'm blessed to be a part of me and you
    I couldn't walk, walk away from you
    Couldn't walk away, couldn't walk away
    I couldn't walk, walk away from you
    Couldn't walk away, couldn't walk away
    Couldn't walk away, couldn't walk away

I had to stay, I could see no other way
To be happy in a big wide lonely land
A man with no woman, woman with no man
Love is happiness and my obsession
Lack or loss thereof will cause depression
    I couldn't walk, walk away from you
    Couldn't walk away, couldn't walk away
    I couldn't walk, walk away from you
    Couldn't walk away, couldn't walk away
    Couldn't walk away, couldn't walk away

326

I'M INSPIRED

(Words & music by Nomi Yah)

He's in the zone before the starting gun
Explodes and shows the world that he can run
See how he rockets through an opening in the crowd
They pile up but he's already out
Push to the limit, that's how to bring it
Until horns sound off across the finish line
    I'm inspired, setting a high bar
    Giving everything to win the race
    There's no second place
    I'm inspired, motivated to try hard
    I'm on fire, I'm inspired

She helps the poor and disadvantaged youth
She volunteers for forty years to do it
She could have given up and gotten out anytime
She lives so they can have a better life
Push to the limit, that's how to bring it
Until horns sound off across the finish line
    I'm inspired, setting a high bar
    Giving everything to win the race
    There's no second place
    I'm inspired, motivated to try hard
    I'm on fire, I'm inspired

To my hero, my example
I say thank you, thank you, thank you, thank you
    I'm inspired, setting a high bar
    Giving everything to win the race
    There's no second place
    I'm inspired, motivated to try hard
    I'm on fire, I'm inspired
    I'm inspired

IF YOU'RE ALIVE

(Words & music by Nomi Yah

If you're alive, send a message, dial a telephone
Five-five-five-seven-one-oh-six, same number as before
Last I heard they found your car in north Mexico
If you're alive, let me know
    Did you make it through the hard times
    Did it all turn out OK
    I never did forget you
    And I wonder to this day
    If you're alive, if you're alive

You got paranoid, saying that we had to leave at dawn
Or be destroyed, were you high or crazy or both
What the hell went wrong
Last time you were ever seen, you were begging me to go
Looking annoyed I said no
    Did you make it through the hard times
    Did it all turn out OK
    I never did forget you
    And I wonder to this day
    If you're alive, if you're alive

You're a dot dot dot
An unfinished thought thought thought
I can't seem to let this go
I just have to know
    If you're alive, if you're alive
    If you're alive

PERFECT ENOUGH

(By Nomi Yah

Your child gets tall while you are busy
Think of it isn't it really a shame
If you miss it all, childhood is brief
Picture books and loose teeth, and that Little League game
Man, relax
> Life is perfect enough, perfect enough
> Lord, it could be better
> Sometimes it's rough
> But today is perfect enough

Your Jaguar's fast, but you're running late
You won't catch the plane, but you'll get on the next
And you'll fly first-class, trying to achieve
The American Dream while you pile up debts
Man, relax
> Life is perfect enough, perfect enough
> Lord, it could be better
> Sometimes it's rough
> But today is perfect enough

You should be proud of what you've done
Look how far you've come

It's all a matter of priority, keep up what you're doing
If it doesn't ruin the time that you spend
With your family, you are their rock
And they love when you walk through that door at the end
Of the day
> Life is perfect enough, perfect enough
> Lord, it could be better
> Sometimes it's rough
> But today is perfect enough

329

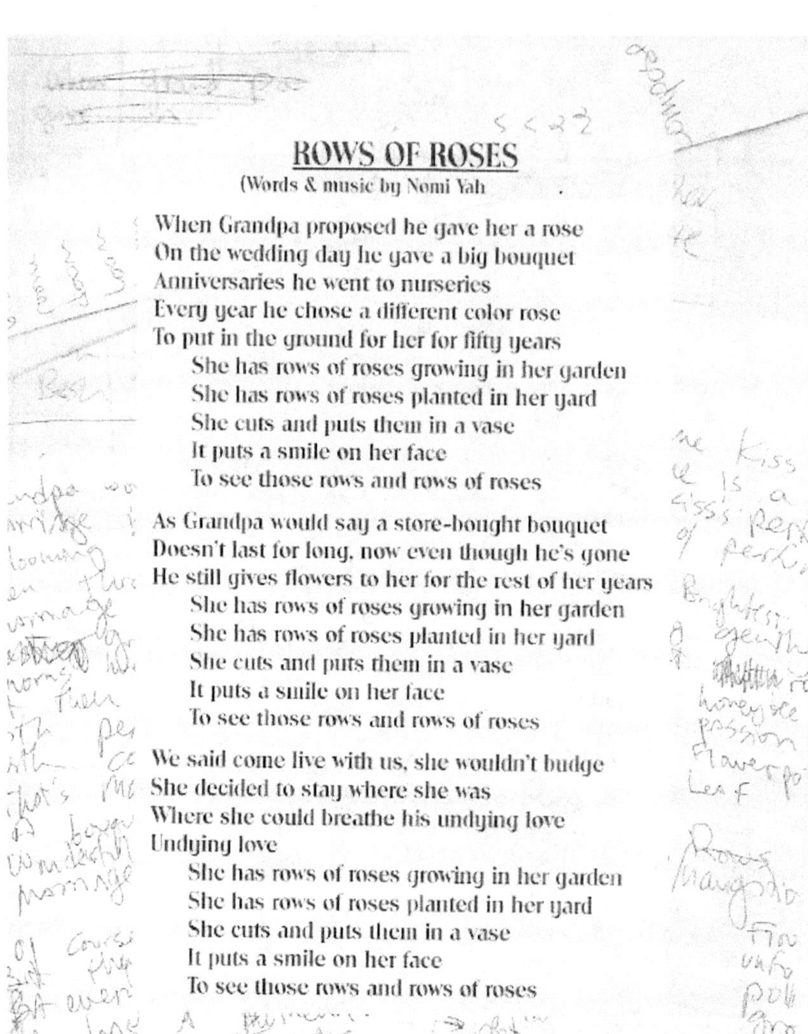

ROWS OF ROSES
(Words & music by Nomi Yah)

When Grandpa proposed he gave her a rose
On the wedding day he gave a big bouquet
Anniversaries he went to nurseries
Every year he chose a different color rose
To put in the ground for her for fifty years
    She has rows of roses growing in her garden
    She has rows of roses planted in her yard
    She cuts and puts them in a vase
    It puts a smile on her face
    To see those rows and rows of roses

As Grandpa would say a store-bought bouquet
Doesn't last for long, now even though he's gone
He still gives flowers to her for the rest of her years
    She has rows of roses growing in her garden
    She has rows of roses planted in her yard
    She cuts and puts them in a vase
    It puts a smile on her face
    To see those rows and rows of roses

We said come live with us, she wouldn't budge
She decided to stay where she was
Where she could breathe his undying love
Undying love
    She has rows of roses growing in her garden
    She has rows of roses planted in her yard
    She cuts and puts them in a vase
    It puts a smile on her face
    To see those rows and rows of roses

TAKE A DAY OFF

(Words & music by Nomi Yah

All that stuff you have to do now
Can't it wait until tomorrow
All we ever do is work
Don't you think that we deserve
An occasional time out
We're going to be playing hooky, calling in sick
Doing whatever we need to be together
    Take a day, take a day, take a day off
    It's time for getting in the sun
    It's time for getting nothing done
    Take a day, take a day, take a day off
    We're going to finally get a break
    We're going to finally get to take a day off

Putting E&J in Pepsi
Kicking it and getting tipsy
We'll be acting juvenile
Like it's going out of style
I just love when you're with me
We're going to be playing hooky, calling in sick
Doing whatever we need to be together
    Take a day, take a day, take a day off
    It's time for getting in the sun
    It's time for getting nothing done
    Take a day, take a day, take a day off
    We're going to finally get a break
    We're going to finally get to take a day off

I don't mean to make you delinquent
But I want to say what I'm thinking
    Take a day, take a day, take a day off
    It's time for getting in the sun
    It's time for getting nothing done
    Take a day, take a day, take a day off
    We're going to finally get a break
    We're going to finally get to take a day off

85

331

WHEN IT'S MAGIC

(Words & music by Nomi Yah & Ron Brown)

When it's magic, yeah yeah yeah yeah
When it's magic, yeah yeah yeah yeah

I shredded when I should have filed and broke the fax machine
The boss went off but I didn't mind 'cause it was six-fifteen
I said, Sorry, I wasn't paying attention
My mind is stuck on someone, it's crazy what happens
When it's magic, love appears in thin air
Loneliness disappears
I'm distracted, that's a classic reaction
Yeah yeah yeah yeah
When it's magic, yeah yeah yeah yeah

I was flying down the road, didn't see the stop sign
A cop brought me back to earth, a four hundred dollar fine
I said, Sorry, I wasn't paying attention
My mind is stuck on someone, it's crazy what happens
When it's magic, love appears in thin air
Loneliness disappears
I'm distracted, that's a classic reaction
When it's magic

The experience is so intense
It goes against common sense
When it's magic, love appears in thin air
Loneliness disappears
I'm distracted, that's a classic reaction
Yeah yeah yeah yeah
When it's magic, yeah yeah yeah yeah

My name at birth was Naomi Batya Ginsberg. My first stage name was Naomi Batya, but it was difficult to pronounce. My friends called me Nomi, so I shortened my stage name to Nomi Yah. My married name was Nomi Yah Wanag. On 11/11/11, I remarried and became Nomi Yah Gardiner. My name has changed over time, but my friends still call me Nomi.

nomi чah
S Nomi - S Love Me

"Great writing, solid chorus, verses very very strong."
(Rich E. Blaze, producer at Diane Warren/Realsongs, worked with Ricky Martin, TLC, Bone Thugs, Rod Stewart, Timbaland)

"Lyrics made me say Wow! Knocked me out."
(Pamela Phillips-Oland, songwriter, 3 Grammy nominations, songs recorded by Whitney Houston, Aretha Franklin, Frank Sinatra, Reba McIntyre)

"Really cool idea, lyrics are whoa!"
(Steve Seskin, songwriter, 7 number one hit songs, Grammy nomination, songs recorded by Tim McGraw, Kenny Chesney)

"Melodic and appealing."
(Dale Kawashima, publisher, previously with Sony/ATV, Jobete/Motown, Mercury Records, worked with catalogs of Michael Jackson, Beatles, Joni Mitchell)

"Real nice track, cool hook, very catchy."
(Andre Pessis, songwriter, 16 hit songs, Grammy winner, 13 platinum records, songs recorded by Tim McGraw, Journey, previous President and Governor of the Grammy Association for San Francisco)

"Great song, strong lyrics."
(Scott Matthews, multi-gold and platinum producer, songwriter, worked with Jerry Garcia, Barbra Streisand, Rolling Stones, Eric Clapton, Carlos Santana)

"This song is a masterpiece."
(Larry Batiste, multi-platinum songwriter, previous President Grammy Association for San Francisco)

"Creative! Sweet song! Cool rhymes, very strong song." (Pete Luboff)
"Love it! Yes! Courageous and creative." (Pat Luboff)
(Pat and Pete Luboff, songwriters, authors, songs recorded by Snoop Dogg, Patti LaBelle)

"You've got some outstanding lyric lines here and fresh rhymes. The storytelling is terrific."
(Taxi A&R)

"Absolutely gorgeous melody!"
(Jai Josefs, songwriter, songs recorded by Jose Feliciano, Little Richard)

ABOUT THE AUTHOR Nomi Yah   ·   co-wrote *King Of Kings*, currently with *Universal Music*, recorded by *Petra* on gold album *Petra Praise: The Rock Cries Out*, top 10 on charts for a year, Nomi co-wrote *Prison* with *Eek-A-Mouse on Eeksperience* album. Her music has been featured in films, commercials and TV shows. She currently manages the *West Coast Songwriters* Berkeley Chapter at the *Freight & Salvage*.

ORDER ON AMAZON OR CONTACT PUBLISHER

$20.00
ISBN 978-0-9898580-0-7
52000>

9 780989 858007

NOMI YAH MUSIC

336

APPENDIX 6
BIBLIOGRAPHY

A.P. Jensen
- The Songwriter

Aaron Copland
- What To Listen For In Music

Alex Ross
- The Rest Is Noise: Listening To The Twentieth Century
- Listen To This

Andrea Stolpe
- Popular Lyric Writing: 10 Steps To Effective Storytelling
- Beginning Songwriting: Writing Your Own Lyrics, Melodies And Chords (coauthor Jan Stolpe)

Andy Hill
- Scoring The Screen: The Secret Language Of Film Music

Anthony Savona
- Console Confessions: The Great Music Producers In Their Own Words

Barbara Ann Kipfer
- Roget's Thesaurus

Barbara L. Jordan
- Songwriter's Playground: Innovative Exercises In Creative Songwriting

Barbara Schultz
- Music Producers: Conversations With Today's Top Hitmakers

Becca Puglisi
- The Emotion Thesaurus: A Writer's Guide To Character Expression

Beth Denisch

- Contemporary Counterpoint: Theory And Application

Bill Flanagan

- Written In My Soul: Conversations With Rock's Great Songwriters

Bill Gordon

- It's Music, Not Theory, Damn It!

Billy Seidman

- The Elements Of Songcraft: The Contemporary Songwriter's Usage Guide To Writing Songs That Last

Bobby Borg

- The Musician's Handbook: A Practical Guide To Understanding The Music Business

Brian Oliver

- How (Not) To Write A Hit Song: 101 Common Mistakes To Avoid For Songwriting Success

Cliff Goldmacher

- The Reason For The Rhymes: Mastering The Seven Essential Skills Of Innovation By Learning To Write Songs

Dan Kimpel

- How They Made It: True Stories Of How Music's Biggest Stars Went From Start To Stardom
- It All Begins With The Music: Developing Successful Artists For The New Music Business (coauthor Don Grierson)
- Networking In The Music Business: Making The Contacts You Need To Succeed In The Music Business

David Naggar, Jeffrey D. Brandstetter

- The Music Business Explained In Plain English: What Every Artist & Songwriter Should Know To Avoid Getting Ripped Off

Dean Krippaehne

- Demystifying The Cue: Thoughts And Strategies For Creating Competitive Film And TV Music In Today's New Media World

Diana Sward Rapaport, Loreena McKennitt
- How To Make And Sell Your Own Recording: The Complete Guide To Independent Recording

Dick Weissman
- Creating Melodies: A Songwriter's Guide To Understanding, Writing And Polishing Melodies

Donald S. Passman
- All You Need To Know About The Music Business

Dude McLean
- The Songwriter's Survival Guide To Success: How To Pitch Your Songs

Ed Bell
- How To Write A Song (Even If You've Never Written One Before And You Think You Suck)
- The Art Of Songwriting: How To Create, Think And Live Like A Songwriter

Edward W. Said
- Music At The Limit

Eric Beall
- The Billboard Guide To Writing And Producing Songs That Sell: How To Create Hits In Today's Music Industry

Ferdinand Davis, Donald Lybbert
- The Essentials Of Counterpoint

Fredric Dannen
- Hit Men

Friedemann Findeisen
- The Addiction Formula: A Holistic Approach To Writing Captivating, Memorable Hit Songs

Greg Forest
- The Music Business Contract Library

Hank Linderman
- Hot Tips For The Home Recording Studio

Herbie Hancock
- Possibilities

Ian Bessler
- Songwriter's Market: Where & How To Market Your Songs

- Songwriting For Dummies: Proven Techniques For Songwriting Success

Jimmy Kachulis
- The Songwriter's Workshop: Melody
- The Songwriter's Workshop: Harmony

Jimmy Webb
- Tunesmith: Inside The Art Of Songwriting

John Bartlett
- Bartlett's Familiar Quotations

John Braheny
- The Craft And Business Of Songwriting: A Practical Guide To Creating And Marketing Artistically and Commercially Successful Songs

John Seabrook
- The Song Machine: Inside The Hit Factory

Katherine Charlton
- Rock Music Styles: A History

Kenny Kerner
- Going Pro: Developing A Professional Career In The Music Industry

Kent J. Klavens
- Protecting Your Songs And Yourself: The Songwriter's Legal Guide

Lamont Dozier
- How Sweet It Is: A Songwriter's Reflections On Music, Motown And The Mystery Of The Muse

Lee Pincus
- The Songwriter Success Manual

Lisa Aschmann
- 1,000 Songwriting Ideas

M. William Krasilovsky, Sidney Shemel
- This Business Of Music: A Practical Guide To The Music Industry For Publishers, Writers, Record Companies, Producers, Artists, Agents

Marc Ferrari
- Rockstar 101: A Rockstar's Guide To Survival And Success In The Music Business

Mark Cawley

- Song Journey: A Hit Songwriter's Guide Through The Process, The Perils And The Payoff Of Writing Songs For A Living

Mark Northam, Lisa Anne Miller
- Film And Television Composer's Resource Guide: The Complete Guide To Organizing And Building Your Business

Martin H. Manser
- Synonyms And Antonyms

Marty Dodson, Bill O'Hanlon
- Song Building: Mastering Lyric Writing
- The Songwriter's Guide To Mastering Co-Writing (coauthor Clay Mills)

Matt Wilson
- Hooks: Lessons On Performance, Business And Life From A Working Musician

Michael Paul Stavrou
- Mixing With Your Mind: Closely Guarded Secrets Of Sound Balance Engineering Revealed

Molly-Ann Leikin
- How To Make A Good Song A Hit Song: Rewriting And Marketing Your Lyrics And Music

Moses Avalon
- Confessions Of A Record Producer: How To Survive The Scams And Shams Of The Music Business
- Million Dollar Mistakes: Steering Your Music Career Clear Of Lies, Cons, Catastrophes And Landmines

Nelson George
- Seduced: A Novel
- The Plot Against Hip-Hop
- The Accidental Hunter

Nicholas Dobson, Karl Coryat
- The Frustrated Songwriter's Handbook: A Radical Guide To Cutting Loose, Overcoming Blocks, And Writing The Best Songs Of Your Life

Nicholas Edwin Renton
- Metaphorically Speaking: A Dictionary Of 3,800 Picturesque Idiomatic Expressions

Pamela Phillips Oland
- The Art Of Writing Great Lyrics

Pat Luboff, Pete Luboff
- 101 Songwriting Wrongs And How To Right Them: How To Craft And Sell Your Songs

Pat Pattison
- Writing Better Lyrics: The Essential Guide To Powerful Songwriting
- Songwriting: Essential Guide To Lyric Form And Structure, Tools And Techniques For Writing Better Lyrics
- Songwriting Without Boundaries: Lyric Writing Exercises For Finding Your Voice
- Songwriting Essential Guide To Rhyming: A Step-By-Step Guide To Better Rhyming And Lyrics

Paul Edwards
- How To Rap: The Art And Science Of The Hip-Hop MC
- How To Rap 2: Advanced Flow And Delivery Techniques

Paul Zollo
- Songwriters On Songwriting

Phillip Furia
- The Poets Of Tin Pan Alley: A History Of America's Great Lyricists

Ralph Murphy
- Murphy's Laws Of Songwriting

Randy Poe
- Music Publishing, A Songwriter's Guide: Everything You Need To Know To Make The Best Publishing Deals For Your Songs

Richard Davis
- Complete Guide To Film Scoring: The Art And Business Of Writing Music For Movies And TV

Richard Jay
- How To Get Your Music In Film And TV

Richard Stim
- Music Law: How To Run Your Band's Business

Steve Winogradsky
- Music Publishing: The Complete Guide

Sue Young
- The New Comprehensive American Rhyming Dictionary

Tara A. Horton
- Songwriter's Market: 2,000 Places To Market Your Songs

Todd Brabec, Jeff Brabec
- Music, Money And Success: The Insider's Guide To Making Money In The Music Business
- Music, Money, Success And The Movies: The Basics Of "Music In Film" Deals

Tom Hall
- The Songwriter's Handbook

Wayne Chase
- How Music Really Works: The Essential Handbook For Songwriters, Performers And Music Students

ABOUT THE COVER ARTIST

BARBARA ANN KLATT (July 5, 1957 - April 23, 2018) was born in Corpus Christi, Texas. At UT Austin, she got a degree in advertising, when her family wouldn't let her major in art. In 1979, she studied in London, where she was introduced to punk rock. In 1981, she moved to San Francisco, becoming roommates with Nomi Yah. Always an avid painter, Barbara also worked as a taxi driver and a security guard. She was employed at the Asian Art Museum, DeYoung and Legion of Honor. She taught English in Beijing for several years, until health problems brought her back to San Francisco.

ABOUT THE AUTHOR

NOMI YAH is a songwriter and author. She co-wrote *King Of Kings* by Petra and Prison by Eek-A-Mouse. Her songs have been signed with Universal, Capitol and EMI. She performed for 25 years, touring internationally. She authored *Notes To Notes: How I Went From Music To Real Estate* and *Writing Lyrics In A Grid*. Nomi lives in Sonoma, California.

www.ingramcontent.com/pod-product-compliance
Lightning Source LLC
Chambersburg PA
CBHW061742250726
48657CB00001B/11